Microsoft® Project 2010

Level 1

Microsoft® Project 2010: Level 1

Part Number: 084602
Course Edition: 1.0

NOTICES

Microsoft® Project 2010: Level 1

About This Course

Project planning and scheduling is a complex task. You may perform various tasks such as gathering information, assigning the appropriate resources required, and planning the budget and overall cost of the project. Microsoft® Project 2010 acts as a tool that assists you in managing all aspects of your projects. In this course, you will create and modify a project plan.

Regardless of job title, most of us have, at one time or another, performed the tasks of a project manager. If you have ever been responsible for coordinating a variety of tasks that had to be completed within a specific time frame for a set amount of money, you have acted as a project manager. You also know, then, that keeping track of all of the project details, such as tasks, resources, and costs, while continuing to focus on the project goals, can be quite a challenge. Whether you are a trained Project Management Professional (PMP), a resource manager, or a team member, Microsoft® Project 2010 can assist you in managing your projects by storing project information, calculating and maintaining the project schedule, tracking project costs, and analyzing and communicating project data.

Course Description

Target Student

This course is designed for a person who has an understanding of project management concepts, who is responsible for creating and modifying project plans, and who needs a tool to manage those project plans.

Course Prerequisites

Students enrolling in this class should have the following:

- A general introductory-level understanding of project management concepts. Courses that help fulfill this requirement include: *Project Management Fundamentals (Second Edition).*

- Basic end-user skills with any current Windows operating system. Courses that help fulfill this requirement include: *Microsoft® Windows® XP Professional: Level 1* or *Microsoft® Windows® Vista™: Level 1* or *Microsoft® Windows® 7: Level 1.*

Course Objectives

In this course, you will create and manage a project schedule using Microsoft® Project 2010.

You will:

- Identify the basic features and components of the Microsoft Project environment.
- Create a new project plan file and enter project information.
- Manage tasks by organizing tasks and setting task relationships.
- Manage resources for a project.
- Finalize a project plan.
- Identify additional methods to create a project schedule in Microsoft Project 2010.

How to Use This Book

As a Learning Guide

This book is divided into lessons and topics, covering a subject or a set of related subjects. In most cases, lessons are arranged in order of increasing proficiency.

The results-oriented topics include relevant and supporting information you need to master the content. Each topic has various types of activities designed to enable you to practice the guidelines and procedures as well as to solidify your understanding of the informational material presented in the course.

At the back of the book, you will find a glossary of the definitions of the terms and concepts used throughout the course. You will also find an index to assist in locating information within the instructional components of the book.

In the Classroom

This book is intended to enhance and support the in-class experience. Procedures and guidelines are presented in a concise fashion along with activities and discussions. Information is provided for reference and reflection in such a way as to facilitate understanding and practice.

Each lesson may also include a Lesson Lab or various types of simulated activities. You will find the files for the simulated activities along with the other course files on the enclosed CD-ROM. If your course manual did not come with a CD-ROM, please go to **http://elementkcourseware.com** to download the files. If included, these interactive activities enable you to practice your skills in an immersive business environment, or to use hardware and software resources not available in the classroom. The course files that are available on the CD-ROM or by download may also contain sample files, support files, and additional reference materials for use both during and after the course.

As a Teaching Guide

Effective presentation of the information and skills contained in this book requires adequate preparation. As such, as an instructor, you should familiarize yourself with the content of the entire course, including its organization and approaches. You should review each of the student activities and exercises so you can facilitate them in the classroom.

Throughout the book, you may see Instructor Notes that provide suggestions, answers to problems, and supplemental information for you, the instructor. You may also see references to "Additional Instructor Notes" that contain expanded instructional information; these notes appear in a separate section at the back of the book. Microsoft® PowerPoint® slides may be provided in the included course files, which are available on the enclosed CD-ROM or by download from **http://elementkcourseware.com**. The slides are also referred to in the text. If you plan to use the slides, it is recommended to display them during the corresponding content as indicated in the Instructor Notes in the margin.

The course files may also include assessments for the course, which can be administered diagnostically before the class, or as a review after the course is completed. These exam-type questions can be used to gauge the students' understanding and assimilation of course content.

As a Review Tool

Any method of instruction is only as effective as the time and effort you, the student, are willing to invest in it. In addition, some of the information that you learn in class may not be important to you immediately, but it may become important later. For this reason, we encourage you to spend some time reviewing the content of the course after your time in the classroom.

As a Reference

The organization and layout of this book make it an easy-to-use resource for future reference. Taking advantage of the glossary, index, and table of contents, you can use this book as a first source of definitions, background information, and summaries.

Course Icons

Icon	Description
	A **Caution Note** makes students aware of potential negative consequences of an action, setting, or decision that are not easily known.
	Display Slide provides a prompt to the instructor to display a specific slide. Display Slides are included in the Instructor Guide only.
	An **Instructor Note** is a comment to the instructor regarding delivery, classroom strategy, classroom tools, exceptions, and other special considerations. Instructor Notes are included in the Instructor Guide only.
	Notes Page indicates a page that has been left intentionally blank for students to write on.
	A **Student Note** provides additional information, guidance, or hints about a topic or task.
	A **Version Note** indicates information necessary for a specific version of software.

Course Requirements

Hardware

You will need one computer for each student and the instructor. To use Microsoft Project 2010 on each machine, you need the following hardware:

- Intel® Pentium® 1.64 MHz or higher processor.
- 512 megabytes (MB) of RAM or more.
- 6 gigabytes (GB) of available hard-disk space or more.
- CD-ROM drive.
- Super VGA or higher resolution monitor. Preferred monitor is a wide screen LCD for viewing Project.
- Microsoft® Mouse, Microsoft® IntelliMouse®, or a compatible pointing device.
- Projection system to display the instructor's computer screen.

Software

Software required on each machine includes the following:

- Microsoft® Project Professional 2010
- Microsoft® Windows® XP Professional with Service Pack 3 or Microsoft® Windows® Vista™ Business Edition or Microsoft® Windows® 7.

    This course was developed using the Microsoft® Windows® XP operating system; however, the manufacturer's documentation states that the Microsoft Project 2010 application will also run on Windows Vista or Windows 7. If you use Windows Vista or Windows 7, you may notice slight differences when keying the course.

Class Setup

Install Windows XP

1. Install Windows XP Professional on an empty partition.

    - Leave the Administrator password blank.
    - For all other installation parameters, use values that are appropriate for your environment (see your local network administrator for details).

2. On Windows XP Professional, disable the **Welcome** screen. (This step ensures that students will be able to log on as the Administrator user regardless of what other user accounts exist on the computer.)

    a. Click **Start** and choose **Control Panel→User Accounts.**

    b. Click **Change The Way Users Log On And Off.**

    c. Uncheck **Use Welcome Screen.**

    d. Click **Apply Options.**

3. On Windows XP Professional, install Service Pack 3. Use the Service Pack installation defaults.

To make the data files and activity steps valid, please change the system clock date to July 10, 2010.

4. Set the time and date for all computers to July 10, 2010.

5. Provide each student with Administrator rights.

Install and Configure Microsoft Project Professional 2010

To install and configure Microsoft Project Professional 2010:

1. Double-click the **setup.exe** file.

2. Enter the product key and click **Continue.**

3. Accept the license agreement and click **Continue.**

4. Click **Install Now.**

5. Once the installation is complete, click **Close.**

6. Launch **Project 2010,** and in the **Welcome to the 2010 Microsoft Office system** dialog box, click **Next.**

7. Select the **Don't make changes** option to decline the usage of **Microsoft Update** and click **OK.**

8. On the Ribbon, choose **File→Project Options→Trust Center** and then click **Trust Center Settings.** In the left pane, click **Legacy Formats** and select the **Allow loading files with legacy or non default file formats** option and then click **OK** twice to close the project options.

9. Exit Project 2010.

Install Data Files

1. On the course CD-ROM, run the 084602dd.exe self-extracting file. This will install a folder named 084602Data on your C drive. This folder contains all the data files that you will use to complete this course. If your course did not come with a CD-ROM, please go to **http://www.elementk.com/courseware-file-downloads** to download the data files.

2. Verify that file extensions are visible. (In Windows Explorer, choose **Organize→Folder and Search Options** and select the **View** tab. If necessary, deselect the **Hide Extensions For Known File Types** option and click **OK.**)

   In addition to the specific setup procedures needed for this class to run properly, you should also check the Element K Press product support website at **http://support.elementkcourseware.com** for more information. Any update about this course will be posted there.

List of Additional Files

Printed with each activity is a list of files students open to complete that activity. Many activities also require additional files that students do not open, but are needed to support the file(s) students are working with. These supporting files are included with the student data files on the course CD-ROM or data disk. Do not delete these files.

1 | Getting Started with Microsoft Project

Lesson Time: 45 minutes

Lesson Objectives:

In this lesson, you will identify the basic features and components of the Microsoft Project environment.

You will:

- Identify the components of the Microsoft Project 2010 user interface.
- Display an existing project plan in different views.

Introduction

If you are responsible for managing a project, then in the planning phases of the project, you would have created many documents, such as a project charter, a team charter, or a statement of work. With this project planning phase complete, you are now ready to create a project plan, and this requires you to be familiar with the features and functions of the project management tool you will use; in this case, Microsoft Project 2010. In this lesson, you will discover the useful features and functions of Microsoft Project 2010.

For a project to be successful, you need to document all information relating to it in an electronic form, so that data can be analyzed and processed automatically. If you do not know how to use an electronic application for your project management tasks, you will not be able to make the best use of your software tool. This will reduce the chances of executing your projects efficiently or professionally. Your familiarity with the features and functions of Microsoft Project 2010 will help you analyze project information accurately, reduce your manual effort, and reduce your risk of errors.

TOPIC A

Explore the Microsoft Project 2010 Environment

If you are going to use Microsoft Project 2010 as your project-management tool, you have probably already installed it on your computer. However, if you are new to Microsoft Project, a good first step is to launch the application and explore the interface and its functions before you begin using it to develop live project plans. In this topic, you will identify the components of the Microsoft Project 2010 environment.

If you purchase a new device without knowing about its various features and their operation, you will not be able to use the device. Similarly, it is essential to identify the various elements of any new application you are using for the first time. By identifying the different components in the Microsoft Project 2010 interface, you can be at ease with its features and functions and then work more efficiently on your project plan files.

Project Management

Definition:

Project management is the application of knowledge, skills, tools, and techniques to project activities, to meet the requirements of a project. This is done by integrating the various standard project management processes, such as initiation, planning, execution, monitoring, controlling, and closing. A *project manager* is responsible for accomplishing the goals of a project by ensuring that work activities are completed as required on time, with quality and within budget.

Example: Project Managers' Responsibilities

Project managers' responsibilities include communicating cross functionally, managing the efforts of people who do not report directly to them, and delivering the work on time, within the allotted budget, and within the specifications for quality.

The Project Management Process

Although each project is unique, there are certain phases that every project should undergo in its life cycle.

Phase	Activity
Initiation	Defining and scoping a project, identifying stakeholders, and building a team.
Planning	Budgeting, scheduling, and planning activities.
Execution	Performing tasks according to the plan and adapting specifications and plans to the stakeholders' expectations.
Monitoring & Controlling	Monitoring progress; balancing the demands of scope, time, and quality; tracking corrective actions; and reporting progress.
Closing	Handing off to end users, closing down operations, and reporting outcomes.

Microsoft Project 2010

Microsoft Project 2010 is a project management application that contains a set of tools to help managers plan, schedule, and control their projects. This software is used to create a project plan file that acts as a repository for all project-related information, including the task list, resources, calendar information, and cost data.

 When you save a Microsoft Project plan file, the file gets stored with the .mpp extension.

Microsoft Project Components

Microsoft Project 2010 provides a well-organized environment with easy access to the tools necessary to efficiently create a project plan.

Interface Component	Description
The Quick Access toolbar	Provides access to commonly used commands such as save, undo, and redo. The toolbar can be customized in the **Project Options** dialog box to suit any user needs and can be moved within the Project environment.
The Ribbon	Provides users with easy access to commonly used tools used to build and manage projects.

Interface Component	Description
The Backstage view	Functions similarly to the previous versions' **File** menu. This view includes common tools available on the traditional **File** menu, such as **Save As, Close,** and the Project **Options** function. 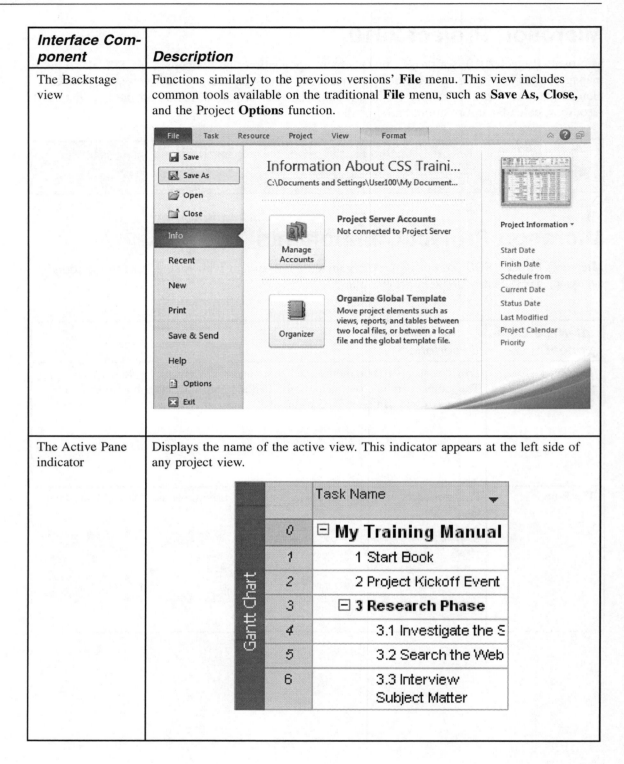
The Active Pane indicator	Displays the name of the active view. This indicator appears at the left side of any project view.

Interface Component	Description
The view area	Displays project data. The **Gantt Chart** view is the default view.
The table	Shows specific information about tasks, resources, and assignments as a set of fields in a view. There are different tables; the **Task Entry** table is displayed in the default view.
The field heading	The field heading is the gray area at the top of each column of the table that indicates the function of each column.
The timescale	Contains the legends that indicate the range of time for graphically presented tasks or resources.

Interface Component	Description
The status bar	The status bar is located at the bottom of the Project environment, and includes: • Cell Mode, which displays whether the cell is in Ready Mode or Enter (Edit) Mode. • Task Mode, which displays whether the task entered is automatically or manually scheduled. • Views options, which include buttons to switch to the **Gantt Chart,** the **Task Usage,** the **Team Planner,** or the **Resource Sheet** view. • The View slider, which is used to quickly zoom in and out of the time phased portion of a view. Ready New Tasks : Auto Scheduled ⊟

The Divide bar	Separates the table and chart portions of a view. It can be dragged to alter what is visible in the view area.
	
	Task Name ar 4, '12 Apr 15, '12
	   S W S T
	⊟ CSS Training Manual
	  ⊟ Research Phase
	    Investigate the Software
	    Search the Web
	    Interview Subject Matter E
	  ⊟ Outline Phase

The Ribbon

The *Ribbon* is a panel at the top portion of the Project environment that contains a selection of easy-to-browse commands that you will use while working in Project. It has several tabs that are divided into logical groups containing features designed to perform specific tasks. The Ribbon can be customized easily to meet end-user or business needs.

ScreenTips

A *ScreenTip* is a label that appears when the mouse pointer is placed over a tool. In Microsoft Project, ScreenTips include a description of the task performed by the tool. This feature helps users identify the functionality of the features and commands that they are not familiar with.

Benefits of the Ribbon

Most of the commands and controls in Microsoft Project are accessible from the Ribbon, rather than through menus and dialog boxes. The Ribbon helps users identify desired functions and perform both simple and advanced operations without having to navigate extensively.

Ribbon Tabs

In Project, the Ribbon contains six tabs organized by user action.

Tab	Description
File	Displays the Backstage view of Project. 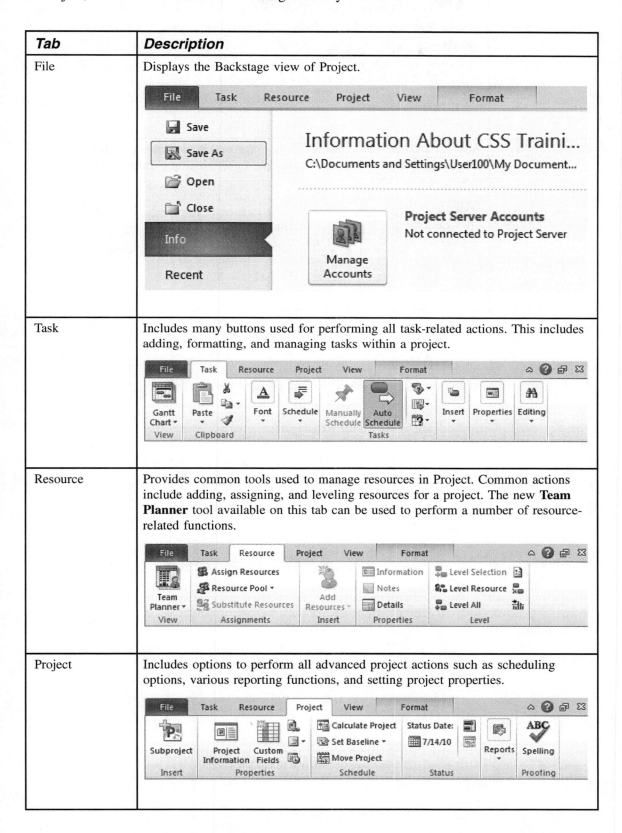
Task	Includes many buttons used for performing all task-related actions. This includes adding, formatting, and managing tasks within a project.
Resource	Provides common tools used to manage resources in Project. Common actions include adding, assigning, and leveling resources for a project. The new **Team Planner** tool available on this tab can be used to perform a number of resource-related functions.
Project	Includes options to perform all advanced project actions such as scheduling options, various reporting functions, and setting project properties.

Tab	Description
View	Includes a number of viewing options available in Project. This tab also includes the new **Timeline** view option. This view option provides useful features that can be used when you need to provide a summary or overview of a project plan.
Format	Provides a variety of formatting options. The options available on this tab will change according to what view is displayed and what formatting options can be applied.

ACTIVITY 1-1

Identifying the Elements of the Microsoft Project Interface

Data Files:

C:\084602Data\Getting Started\CSS Training Manual.mpp

Scenario:

You are the project manager for your company; you have been assigned your first project. Your manager suggests that you familiarize yourself with the Project application before the project kick-off meeting.

1. Launch Microsoft Office Project 2010 and open the CSS Training Manual.mpp file in its default view.

   a. On the Windows taskbar, choose **Start→Microsoft Project 2010** to launch the application.

   b. On the Ribbon, choose **File→Open.**

   c. In the **Open** dialog box, in the **Look in** pane, click **My Computer.**

   d. Navigate to C:\084602Data\ and double-click the **Getting Started** folder.

   e. In the file list area, select the **CSS Training Manual.mpp** file and click **Open.**

2. Examine the tabs on the Microsoft Project Ribbon.

   a. Notice that the **Task** tab is displayed by default, and review the options available on the tab.

   b. In the **Properties** section, click the **Information** button to view the **Summary Task Information** dialog box.

   c. Review the options available to set for summary tasks within a project and then click **Cancel.**

   d. In the table, select the **Search the Web** task and view the information.

   e. On the Ribbon, click the **Resource** tab.

   f. Review all the options available to manage resources within a project, and on the Ribbon, click the **Project** tab.

   g. Review the options available to manage at the project level, and on the Ribbon, click the **View** tab.

h. In the **Task Views** section, click the **Task Usage** button to switch views.

i. On the **View** tab, click **Gantt Chart** to switch back to the **Gantt** view.

j. On the Ribbon, click the **Format** tab and then review the format options available for the **Gantt** chart.

TOPIC B

Display an Existing Project Plan in Different Views

Now that you have identified the components of the Microsoft Project 2010 environment, you are ready to examine the project plans themselves. In the Project environment, there are various views in which you can work based on your need. In this topic, you will display an existing project plan in different views.

Let's suppose that you had to describe to your client the budgetary allocation for every phase of a project. It would be more effective if you could show the budget breakdown in a pie chart rather than showing the timeline for the project. Because different kinds of project information require different kinds of presentation, Microsoft Project helps you communicate project information effectively through multiple project views.

Microsoft Project Views

Microsoft Project 2010 provides various task, resource, and assignment views on the **View** tab. These views display an information subset by using different formats and components.

View Type	Used To
Calendar	Create, edit, show, or review tasks scheduled on specific days, weeks, or months in a calendar.
Gantt Chart	View tasks and associated information in a sheet, and observe tasks and duration over time in a bar graph on a timescale. You can also use this view type to enter and schedule a list of tasks. This view appears by default in Project.
Network Diagram	Enter, edit, and review all tasks and task dependencies in a project. You can also use this view type to create and fine tune your schedule in a flowchart format.
Task Usage	Review, enter, and edit assignments by task. The sheet portion of the view has tasks listed with their assigned resources, and the timesheet portion contains information about the tasks such as work or costs according to the timescale.
Tracking Gantt	Compare the baseline schedule with the actual schedule while implementing a project. In this view, you can view the tasks and task information in a sheet, and a chart showing a baseline and scheduled Gantt bars for each task.
Team Planner	Manage resource allocation in the resource list format. In this view, you can view unscheduled tasks by resource and also view all unassigned tasks. This allows you to quickly edit all resource assignments in one view.
Resource Sheet	Enter, edit, and review resource information in a spreadsheet format.
Resource Usage	Review, enter, and edit assignments by resource. The sheet portion of the view contains a list of resources with associated task assignments, and the timesheet portion details the costs or work for the resources on a timescale.

More Views

Besides the commonly used views, Project provides other options for viewing project information with the help of the **More Views** dialog box. Using **More Views,** you can observe relationships across variables such as cost, work, and resources in views such as **Relationship Diagram, Detail Gantt, Descriptive Network Diagram,** and **Resource Allocation.** The **More Views** dialog box can be accessed in a number of ways on the **View** tab by clicking the drop-down arrow on any of the view options.

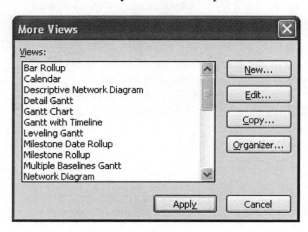

Timescales

Definition:

A *timescale* is the range of time within which work has elapsed. In Microsoft Project, the timescale is the time period indicator that appears at the top of the time-phased portion of various project views. In a project, the timescale helps you identify and define the period during which a task is to be completed or a resource is available.

 In Microsoft Project, timescale appears as an indicator in various project views, such as **Gantt Chart, Task Usage,** and **Resource Usage.**

Example:

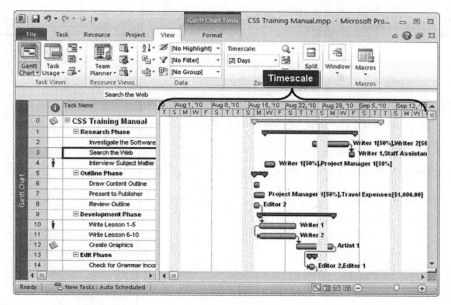

Figure 1-1: *A sample timescale.*

How to Display an Existing Project Plan in Different Views

Procedure Reference: Open an Existing Project Plan

To open an existing project plan:

1. Launch the Microsoft Project 2010 application.

   - Choose **Start→All Programs→Microsoft Office→Microsoft Project 2010** or;

   - On the desktop, double-click the **Microsoft Project 2010** icon.

2. Display the **Open** dialog box.

   - On the Ribbon, choose **File→Open** or;

   - On the keyboard, press **Ctrl+O.**

3. In the **Open** dialog box, navigate to the location of the folder that contains the project plan.

4. Open the project plan.

   - In the file list area, select the appropriate .mpp file and click **Open** or;

   - In the file list area, double-click the file.

Procedure Reference: Display an Existing Plan in Different Project Views

To display an existing plan in different views:

1. Open the project file you want to view.

2. On the **View** tab, select a view to display the project plan.

You can also access all the view options on the **Task** tab in the **Views** section by clicking the **Gantt Chart** drop-down list.

3. If desired, display the project plan by using a view in the **More Views** dialog box.

   a. On the **View** tab, click any view drop-down arrow and select **More Views.**

   b. Display the desired view.

      ● In the **Views** list box, double-click the desired view or;

      ● Select a view and click **Apply.**

4. Save the project plan file to save the view.

ACTIVITY 1-2
Displaying a Project File in Different Views

Before You Begin:
The CSS Training Manual.mpp file is open.

Scenario:
The project management team at your company uses Microsoft Project 2010 to create, monitor, and implement project plans. You have newly joined the team as a project lead. You need to know the various formats available for viewing information. You are asked to look at the CSS Training Manual.mpp file and then view information related to tasks and resources.

1. Display the file in different views.

   a. On the Ribbon, click the **View** tab and then in the **Resource Views** section, click **Resource Sheet.** The Resource Sheet enables you to enter and edit resource information.

   b. On the **View** tab, in the **Task Views** section, click **Network Diagram**  to view project tasks and task dependencies.

   c. The Network Diagram shows you project tasks and task dependencies. To compare views, on the **View** tab, in the **Task Views** section, click **Task Usage.**

2. Display the **Team Planner** view.

   a. Once you have reviewed the **Task Usage** view, in the **Resource Views** section of the **View** tab, click the **Team Planner** button.

b.   This view provides a breakdown of tasks assigned by resource and allows you to assign tasks within the view. Click the **Gantt Chart** button to switch back to the default view.

c.   Choose **File**→**Close** to close the file.

d.   In the **Microsoft Project** dialog box, click **No.**

Lesson 1 Follow-up

In this lesson, you identified the features and functions of the Microsoft Project 2010 environment, including various project views. Acquainting yourself with the components of the Project interface helps you efficiently complete your projects.

1. **Compared to the project management tools you are used to working with, how do you think Microsoft Project can enhance your approach to planning in project management?**

2. **While exploring the Microsoft Project environment, what components did you find the most useful for your type of work?**

2 | Creating a Project Plan

Lesson Time: 1 hour(s), 45 minutes

Lesson Objectives:

In this lesson, you will create a new project plan file and enter project information.

You will:

- Create a project plan file.
- Assign a project calendar.
- Add tasks to a project plan file.
- Enter duration estimates for tasks.
- Add resources to the project plan file.

Introduction

In the previous lesson, you identified the features, functions, and various views of the Project environment. Now, you need to use Project to create an electronic project plan that will contain the complete project-related information, which will be used to work out and follow a project schedule. In this lesson, you will create a project plan, which will include the project start date, project calendar, project tasks and their duration, and the resources involved.

For your project to be successful, it is imperative that you accurately define it within Microsoft Project. This will be easy if you have done all the preliminary work of creating a complete and accurate project plan. If you can accurately enter relevant project information into your project plan, including your company's working schedule, the project tasks, and the project resources, you can build the necessary foundation to help ensure that your project will finish on time, within budget, and within scope.

TOPIC A
Create a Project Plan

In this lesson, you will create a basic project plan with all the structural components you will need to manage the project end to end. The first step in building the structure of the plan is to create an original plan document. In this topic, you will create and save a project plan that contains general project information such as the project start date, the project title, and the project manager's name.

Keeping track of project tasks, resources, costs, and schedules can be an overwhelming task. By entering your approved project plan information into Microsoft Project, you can automate much of your project management efforts by accessing one repository for all your project-related components, as well as stay organized and save time. Creating the actual project plan is the first step in this process.

Project Schedule Creation Methods

In Project 2010, you can use a number of methods to create a project schedule.

Method	Allows You To
Blank project	Create a project plan completely from the beginning. This option does not include any default information, and allows you to build a project plan to meet your specific needs.
Recent templates	Create a project from a template that you have used previously.

Method	Allows You To
 **My templates**	Create a project using any custom built template that you have created and saved. This can also be useful for templates that are created for a specific business need and that are distributed and shared among coworkers.
 **New from existing project**	Start a new project plan from a plan that is already built. This may be useful when you are starting a project that is similar to a completed project, when the prior project is not saved as a template.
 **New from Excel workbook**	Create a project plan by using information that was created in an Excel workbook.
 **New from SharePoint task list**	Create a project plan by using Project Tasks lists that were created in SharePoint.

Method	Allows You To
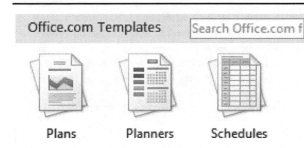 Office.com Templates	Access and use the Office.com project plan templates directly in Project without having to open a web browser.

Microsoft SharePoint

Microsoft SharePoint, also known as Microsoft SharePoint Products and Technologies, is a collaboration and web-publishing software product from Microsoft®. This software enables individuals working on a project team or in a functional group to share information and communicate with one another from a central location. It allows users to work in a web-based collaborative environment. Microsoft SharePoint provides specialized websites that contain elements including a central calendar, task lists, libraries of documents, discussion boards, and various other elements. Team members can access the site via a web browser from their PC or a PDA. SharePoint also integrates seamlessly with Microsoft Office applications in a single environment.

The Project Information Dialog Box

Project scheduling is a key factor in the decision-making process of a project. Using the **Project Information** dialog box, you can schedule your organization's projects and tasks with available resources. If you enter a **Start date** for the project, by default, Project schedules tasks to begin on the project's start date and calculates the project's **Finish date** based on the last task to finish. You can also specify the type of calendar you want to set as your project calendar through the **Calendar** option.

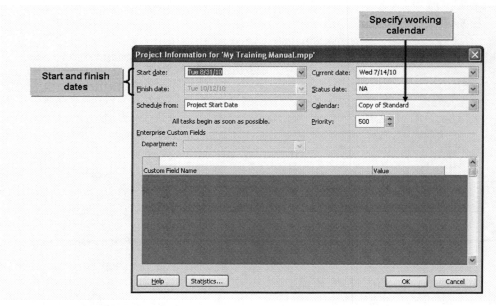

Figure 2-1: *Project information.*

Project Scheduling from a Project End Date

Although most projects will be scheduled from a known start date, there may be times when you are forced to schedule from a finish date. An example of when you will schedule a project from a finish date could be when you have a customer delivery deadline that must be met regardless of when you start the project. To schedule a project from the finish date, in the **Project Information** dialog box, enter the project finish date in the **Finish date** text box. When scheduling from a project finish date, keep in mind that Project will handle some actions very differently.

The Project Properties Dialog Box

The **Project Properties** dialog box provides you with various tabs for entering the general information about a project plan.

Tab	Description
General	Displays various pieces of information, such as the file name, type, size, location of the file and its attributes, about the project.
Summary	Allows you to enter project information such as the manager's name, the name of the company, the subject, and the title of the project.
Statistics	Indicates the access properties, such as the time of creation and modification, of the file.
Contents	Specifies project-level values, such as the start and finish dates, duration of the project, total work hours, cost of the project, and the percentage of work completed.
Custom	Displays project information that can be customized in terms of the person or the department that has verified the document, and other file properties such as the status of completion of work.

The Timescale Dialog Box

The **Timescale** dialog box is used to specify and format the view options for the three tiers or units in a timescale.

Tab	Description
Top Tier	Specifies the default time unit as months for the top timescale tier. This tab appears when you choose to show all the three available tiers.
Middle Tier	Specifies the default time unit as weeks for the middle timescale tier. This tab appears when you choose to show at least two of the three available tiers.
Bottom Tier	Specifies the default time unit as days for the bottom timescale tier. This tab appears when you choose to show any of the three available tiers.
Non-working time	Specifies the options available to format the nonworking time specified in a project schedule.

Tables

Definition:

Tables control the kind of information you want to present about tasks, resources, and assignments in a sheet view. By choosing a table from the **View** menu, you can display various tables and control the columns that appear in the table. Tables display your project data in a horizontal row format, with each task and its related information appearing in a single row. The intersection of a column and a row is called a *cell*. Cells contain the individual pieces of data in the table.

Example:

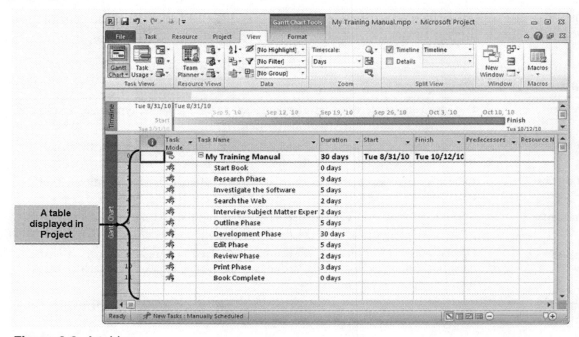

Figure 2-2: A table.

Navigating in Tables

You can use the arrow keys to move from cell to cell in a table, or press **Tab** to move one column to the right. You can also press **Home** to move to the **Indicators** column of the selected row.

Fields

Definition:

A *field* is a location in a sheet, form, or chart that contains a specific information about a task, a resource, or an assignment. It may be a part of a table, a part of a form view, or a timephased area of a usage view. Each column in a table is a separate field. For example, the **Task Entry** table, displayed in the **Gantt Chart** view, displays the **Task Name, Duration, Start, Finish, Predecessors,** and **Resource Names** fields for each task within your project.

Example:

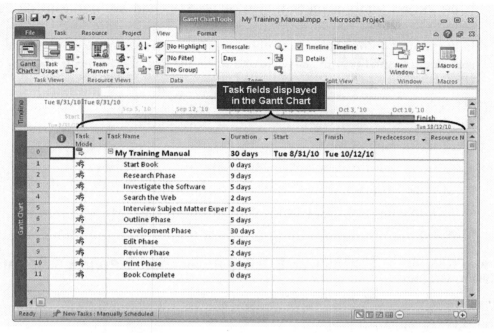

Figure 2-3: Fields in the Gantt Chart view.

Custom Fields

You can customize fields within your project to display specific values or information that is unique to your project. To set a custom field, you can right-click on any column header and choose **Custom Fields.** The **Custom Fields** dialog box includes many options for creating a custom field. Another way to add custom fields to your project is to use the **Add New Column** in the task table.

How to Create a Project Plan File

Procedure Reference: Create a Project Plan

To create a project plan:

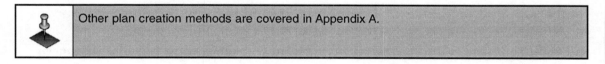

Other plan creation methods are covered in Appendix A.

1. Choose **File→New** to display the new project options.
2. Display a blank new project plan.
   - In the **Available Templates** section, double-click **Blank project** or;
   - In the **Available Templates** section, select **Blank Project,** and in the **Blank project** section, click **Create.**
3. On the Ribbon, on the **Project** tab, open the **Project Information** dialog box.

4. If desired, enter the start date of your project.

- In the **Project Information** dialog box, in the **Start date** text box, enter the desired date in the text box and click **OK** or;

- In the **Project Information** dialog box, from the **Start date** drop-down arrow, navigate to the desired project start date and select the date from the calendar and click **OK.**

5. Save the file.

   a. Display the **Save As** dialog box.

   - Choose **File→Save As** or;

   - On the Quick Access toolbar, click **Save** or;

   - On the keyboard, press **Ctrl+S.**

   b. In the **File name** text box, type the desired name for the file.

   c. Click **Save.**

Procedure Reference: Schedule an Existing Project from a Project Start Date for an Existing Project

To add or change a start date to schedule an existing project from a start date:

1. Open an existing project plan.

2. On the Ribbon, select the **Project** tab and click **Project Information.**

3. From the **Schedule from** drop-down list, select **Project Start Date** to schedule a project from the start date.

4. Enter the start date of the project.

   - In the **Project Information** dialog box, in the **Start date** text box, type the desired start date of the project or;

   - In the **Project Information** dialog box, click the **Start date** drop-down arrow, navigate to the desired start date, and select it.

5. In the **Project Information** dialog box, click **OK** and save the file.

Procedure Reference: Define the Properties of a Project

To define the file properties of a project:

1. Open an existing project plan.

2. On the Ribbon, choose **File** to display the project's **Information** page.

3. In the right pane, click the **Project Information** drop-down arrow and click **Advanced Properties.**

4. On the **Summary** tab, enter the necessary details relevant to the project.

5. Click **OK** to close the **Properties** dialog box.

Procedure Reference: Change the Timescale of a Project

To change the timescale of a project:

1. Open an existing project plan.

2. On the Ribbon, select the **View** tab, and in the **Zoom** section, click the **Days** drop-down arrow and select **Timescale** to display the **Timescale** dialog box.

3. Select the desired tab of the tier you want to modify.

4. In the **Timescale options** section, from the **Show** drop-down list, select the desired change to display the chosen tier level.

5. If necessary, select any other tier tab and make the desired changes.

6. Click **OK** to apply the changes made in the **Timescale** dialog box and save the file.

ACTIVITY 2-1
Creating a Project Plan

Scenario:

You are the project manager for Our Global Company. You are assigned to manage a new project to develop an internal company training manual. The initiation and planning phases of the training manual development project are complete. With a start date of August 31st and some high level project information handed to you by the senior management team, you need to get started by creating a plan in Microsoft Project and entering some general project information.

---

1.   Open a blank project plan.

  a.   On the Ribbon, choose **File→New.**

  b.   Verify that **Blank project** is selected and click **Create.**

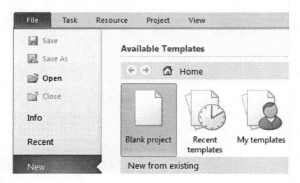

---

2.   Enter the project's start date.

  a.   On the Ribbon, click the **Project** tab and then click **Project Information.**

  b.   From the **Start date** drop-down calendar, click the right arrow to display the **August, 2010** calendar.

  c.   Select the **31st** of August as the start date and click **OK.**

---

3.   Save the project file.

  a.   On the Ribbon, choose **File→Save As.**

  b.   In the **Save As** dialog box, navigate to the C:\084602Data\Creating a Project Plan folder.

  c.   In the **File name** text box, double-click and type *My Training Manual.mpp*

  d.   Click **Save.**

---

4.   Enter the file properties for the project plan.

a. On the Ribbon, click **File** and choose **Project Information**→**Advanced Properties** to display the **My Training Manual.mpp Properties** dialog box.

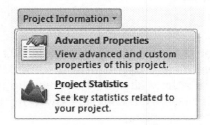

b. On the **Summary** tab, in the **Subject** text box, click and type *Training Manual*

c. In the **Manager** text box, type your name.

d. In the **Company** text box, click and type *Our Global Company*

e. In the **Comments** text box, click and type *Our goal is to market quality products.*

f. Click **OK** and then click the **File** tab to close the Backstage view.

g. On the Quick Access toolbar, click the **Save** button.

TOPIC B
Assign a Project Calendar

In the previous topic, you created and saved a new project plan that included a project start date, but no other scheduling information. For Project to correctly calculate a schedule for the created project, the company's working and nonworking times should be entered into the plan. In this topic, you will create a project calendar that includes your company's working and non-working times, and then assign that calendar to your project plan.

One of the benefits of using Project is that it will create a schedule for all the tasks in your project plan. To ensure that project tasks do not get scheduled to be executed at midnight or on company holidays, you will need to specify and assign a project calendar that includes your company's working and nonworking times.

Base Calendars

A project must base its schedule on some measure of time. Microsoft Project uses *base calendars* to create a schedule for a project. A base calendar is used as a template for scheduling the standard working time, which includes work hours for each day and work days for each week. The base calendar also includes nonworking times and any exception to normal work hours, such as holidays.

 You can also create your own base calendars, which will be useful if you have alternative schedules for multiple resources. For example, you might have resources working part time, 12–hour shifts, or on weekends.

Types of Base Calendars

Project has three default base calendars—**Standard, 24 Hours,** and **Night Shift.**

Base Calendar	Description
Standard	Reflects a traditional work schedule of Monday through Friday, 8:00 A.M. to 5:00 P.M. with a 1-hour break. This is the default base calendar for project, resource, and task calendars.
24 Hours	Reflects a schedule with no nonworking time for projects that are worked on around the clock. This calendar can be used to schedule resources and tasks for different shifts round the clock, or to schedule equipment resources continuously.
Night Shift	Reflects a shift schedule of Monday night through Saturday morning, 11:00 P.M. to 8:00 A.M. with a 1-hour break.

Calendar Types

Project provides various types of calendars to define the working hours or days, and nonworking time for an entire project, or even for individual resources and tasks.

Calendar Type	Description
Project calendar	The base calendar that specifies the default working and nonworking times for a project. The **Standard** base calendar is the default project calendar.
Resource calendar	A calendar created to specify the working and nonworking times for an individual resource when exceptions from the base calendar exist. The **Standard** base calendar is the default resource calendar.
Task calendar	A calendar applied to an individual task created to control the scheduling of a task when exceptions from the base calendar exist. By default, all tasks are scheduled according to the project calendar.

The Change Working Time Dialog Box

The options in the **Change Working Time** dialog box allow you to create, review, and modify the base and project calendars for a project, resource, or task.

Option	Description
For calendar	Provides the available list of base and project calendars for your project.
Legend	Displays an index of colored boxes with a description for each colored box that includes the working, nonworking times, and exception days or hours in your base calendar.
Click on a day to see its working times	Displays a preview of your project calendar with its working times, or any exception on a particular date.
Exceptions	Allows you to set occasional variances to normal working hours, such as holidays and personal time off.
Work Weeks	Allows you to set up the normal week for the selected calendar.
Details	Allows you to specify changes to the days of the week in the **Details** dialog box.
Create New Calendar	Allows you to create a new base calendar for your project using the **Create New Base Calendar** dialog box.

How to Assign a Project Calendar

Procedure Reference: Configure a Project Calendar

To configure a project calendar:

1. Open the desired project plan.

2. If you need to create a calendar, click **Create New Calendar,** and in the **Create New Calendar** dialog box, specify the settings for the new calendar.

   - In the **Name** text box, type the name of the new calendar and select the **Create new base calendar** option and then click **OK** to return to the **Change Working Time** dialog box.

   - If necessary, select the **Make a copy of calendar** option, and from the **Make a copy of calendar** drop-down list, select the desired calendar for making a copy and click **OK.**

3. If the calendar already exists, from the **For calendar** drop-down list, select the calendar you want to change.

4. If you need to change the default work week, click the **Work Weeks** tab.

5. On the **Work Weeks** tab, you can choose or create an additional work week schedule for a range of days that differ from the default work day. In the **Working times** table, type a descriptive name in the **Name** column for the new work week schedule and then enter the start times and the finish times for the time.

6. Click **Details** and make the appropriate changes in the **Details for** dialog box to change working or nonworking days.

   - **Use Project default times for these days.** Choose the days that should use the default working times, which are 8:00 A.M. to 12:00 P.M. and 1:00 P.M. to 5:00 P.M., Monday through Friday, and nonworking time on weekends.

   - **Set days to nonworking time.** Choose the days on which no work can be scheduled. For example, if no one in your organization works on a Friday, select Friday, and then select **Set days to nonworking time.**

   - **Set days to these specific working times.** To set the working times for the selected days throughout the schedule, type the times that you want work to start in the **From** boxes and the times you want work to end in the **To** boxes. For example, if people in your organization work on Saturdays, select Saturday, and then select **Set day(s) to these specific working times.**

7. Click **OK.**

8. If necessary, set changes to the working times of the calendar as exceptions.

   - Select the **Exceptions** tab and in the **Name** column, select the available row and type the name of the exception.

   - Type the **Start** and **Finish** dates, or select the dates from the drop-down calendars for the exception.

   - If necessary, with the exception row still selected, use the **Details** button to specify the nondefault working times or hours for the exception dates.

9. Click **OK** to save the changes made in the **Change Working Time** dialog box.

Procedure Reference: Assign a Calendar to a Project

To assign a calendar to a project:

1. Open the desired project plan and on the Ribbon, on the **Project** tab, click **Project Information.**

2. In the **Project Information** dialog box, from the **Calendar** drop-down list, select the desired calendar.

3. Click **OK.**

ACTIVITY 2-2
Assigning a Calendar to a Project

Before You Begin:
The My Training Manual.mpp file is open.

Scenario:
With your project already created in Microsoft Project, it is important to make sure that you enter any holiday or other company specific functions. The Human Resources department has issued a list of company holidays and time off for the year 2010. As the project manager for the training manual project, you want to ensure that Project considers these company holidays when scheduling your project. Here is the company's holiday list for the timeframe of your project:

- September 6, 2010 (Labor Day)
- November 25 and 26, 2010 (Thanksgiving)
- December 23 and 24, 2010 (Christmas)
- December 21, 2010 (Holiday Luncheon—All employees to work half a day, from 8:00 A.M.–12:00 P.M.)

---

1. Create a calendar named *Our Global Company.*

    a. On the Ribbon, on the **Project** tab, click **Change Working Time.**

    b. Click **Create New Calendar** to display the **Create New Base Calendar** dialog box.

    c. In the **Name** text box, type *Our Global Company*

    d. In the **Make a copy of calendar** drop-down list, verify that the **Standard** base calendar is selected and click **OK.**

    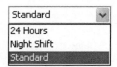

---

2. Specify the company holidays as nonworking days.

    a. On the **Exceptions** tab, select the first row, and in the **Name** column, in the first cell, click and type *Labor Day* and then press **Enter.**

If you would rather use the calendar to set dates in Project, you can select the drop-down arrow in the date text boxes.

b.   In the **Start** column, in the first row, click and type *09/06/2010* and then press **Enter.**

c.   Observe that in the first row, in the **Finish** column, the date **09/06/2010** is auto populated.

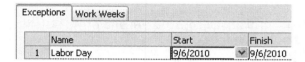

	Name	Start		Finish
1	Labor Day	9/6/2010	⌄	9/6/2010

d.   In the **Click on a day to see its working times** calendar preview, scroll down to **November 2010.**

e.   In the calendar preview, select **25,** hold down **Shift,** and select **26.**

f.   On the **Exceptions** tab, in the **Name** column, in the second row, click and type *Thanksgiving* and then press **Enter.**

	Name	Start	Finish
1	Labor Day	9/6/2010	9/6/2010
2	Thanksgiving	11/25/2010	11/26/2010

g.   In the **Click on a day to see its working times** calendar preview, scroll down to **December 2010.**

h.   In the calendar preview, select **23,** hold down **Shift,** and select **24.**

i.   On the **Exceptions** tab, select the third row, and in the **Name** column, click and type *Christmas* and then press **Enter.**

	Name	Start	Finish
1	Labor Day	9/6/2010	9/6/2010
2	Thanksgiving	11/25/2010	11/26/2010
3	Christmas	12/23/2010	12/24/2010

3.   Specify the nondefault work days.

a.   In the calendar preview, in the month of **December 2010,** select **21.**

b.   Select the **Work Weeks** tab, and in the **Name** column, select the row after the **[Default]** working time row.

	Name	Start	Finish
1	[Default]	NA	NA

c.   In the **Name** column, type *Luncheon* and press **Enter.**

d.   In the **Name** column, select **Luncheon** and click **Details.**

e.   In the **Details for 'Luncheon'** dialog box, in the **Select day(s)** list box, select **Tuesday.**

    f.   Select the **Set day(s) to these specific working times** option to change the day to a half working day.

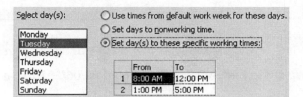

    g.   In the second row, in the **From** column, select **1:00 PM** and press **Delete** to delete the afternoon working hours from 1 PM to 5 PM.

    h.   Click **OK** to close the **Details for 'Luncheon'** dialog box.

    i.   In the **Change Working Time** dialog box, click **OK** to save the changes for the non-working days in the project calendar.

---

4.   Assign the **Our Global Company** calendar to the Training Manual project.

    a.   On the Ribbon, on the **Project** tab, click **Project Information** to display the **Project Information for 'My Training Manual.mpp'** dialog box.

    b.   From the **Calendar** drop-down list, select **Our Global Company.**

    c.   Click **OK.**

    d.   Save the file.

TOPIC C
Add Tasks to a Project Plan

Once you have created a project plan and assigned a project calendar to it, you can add the tasks required to complete your project. In this topic, you will add tasks to a project plan.

In order for your project to be complete, you must enter the tasks needed. Tasks are the building blocks of creating an accurate project plan. If proper tasks are not entered in the beginning phases of project creation, then the project resources and costs assigned to those tasks may also be incorrect. With the right tasks entered in your project, you will be able to better organize the tasks and create the correct dependencies for those tasks.

Tasks

Definition:

A *task* is an individual work item in a project. All tasks contain a **Task Name,** and require an estimated amount of time for execution, known as the duration, which is indicated by the start and finish time. When you enter a task into the project plan, depending on the task mode, Project either assigns a default duration of **1 day?,** with the question mark indicating an estimate, or the duration is left blank.

Example:

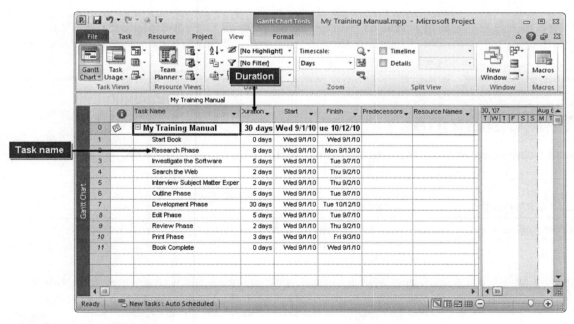

Figure 2-4: A Project task.

Importing a Task List

Task lists can be imported into Microsoft Project from Microsoft Excel and Outlook. You can access the **Excel Import Wizard** using the **Open** dialog box, and you can import tasks from Outlook from the **Task** tab. Task lists can also be pasted directly into a project plan from these applications without having to reformat them afterwards.

Task Modes

Tasks can be entered manually or automatically based on the task information available for your project.

 The default task mode can be changed at any time during a project's lifecycle at the task level, the project level, or even at the application level by configuring the Project options.

Task Mode	Description
Manually Scheduled	Manual mode is the default task mode in Project. It is also known as user-controlled scheduling. This mode enables you to have complete control over the task duration and the start and finish dates. Once a task is entered, these fields are blank and can be populated once the information is known. This mode can be extremely helpful at the beginning stages of creating a project plan when specific task information is not confirmed, but you still want to capture the task in the plan. Manually scheduled tasks are marked with the pushpin icon in the **Task Mode** field of the **Gantt Chart.** In this mode, when you enter a task, the default duration is left blank.
Auto Scheduled	Auto-scheduled mode can be turned on in Project from the **Task** tab for new tasks or by using the **Task mode** drop-down menu to switch the mode of an existing task. This mode enables Project to automatically schedule the task for you based on dependencies, constraints, calendars, and other factors. Automatically scheduled tasks are marked with the Gantt bar icon in the **Task Mode** field of the Gantt Chart. In this mode, when you enter a task, the default duration is populated with a default of **1 day?**

Task Categories

Various categories of tasks are used to identify a task's hierarchical position.

Task Category	Description
Project summary task	Indicates the highest level of work in a project, and represents the project goal or project objective. All other project tasks are represented as subtasks beneath the project summary task.
Summary task	Contains the broad concepts of projects, and is represented in the **Gantt Chart** by black bars with black triangular end points. Summary task start and finish dates do not need to match the subtask dates exactly. This allows more flexibility in the beginning phases of creating a project plan when key dates are not known yet.
Subtask	Contains the detailed steps necessary to complete the summary tasks, and is represented in the **Gantt Chart** as blue bars.

How to Add Tasks to a Project Plan

Procedure Reference: Add Tasks to a Project Plan

To add tasks to a project plan:

1. If necessary, open a project plan in the **Gantt Chart** view.
2. Enter summary tasks.
   a. In the desired row of the **Task** table, select a cell.
   b. On the Ribbon, on the **Task** tab, in the **Insert** section, click the **Insert Summary Task** button.

 Although it makes sense to enter the tasks in the order that they will occur, it is easy to insert and relocate a task within the **Entry** table.

   c. Repeat steps a, b, and c until all the tasks are entered in the project plan.

 If you inadvertently double-click a task name in the **Entry** table, the **Task Information** dialog box is displayed. Click **OK** to close it.

3. Enter subtasks.
   a. In the **Entry** table, select the row underneath where you want to add the new task.
   b. On the Ribbon, on the **Task** tab, click **New Task,** or press **Insert.**
   c. In the **Task Name** field, enter the subtask name.
   d. Repeat steps b and c until all the subtasks for the summary task are entered.

Task Editing Options

It is possible that the tasks in your project plan will change. You can edit existing tasks in many ways. The steps to edit tasks are displayed in the following table.

Edit Result	Procedure
Edit text in a cell	1. Select the task name. 2. Edit one or more characters by using the arrow keys, **Backspace,** and **Delete.** 3. Press **Enter** or click the green check mark.

Edit Result	Procedure
Move or copy a task	1. Select the entire task by clicking the ID number for the task. 2. Cut or copy the task. • On the Ribbon, on the **Task** tab, in the **Clipboard** section, click **Cut** or **Copy** or; • Right-click the ID number and choose **Cut** or **Copy** or; • Press **Ctrl+X** or **Ctrl+C.** 3. Click in the row where you want the task to appear. 4. Paste the task in the new location. • On the Ribbon, on the **Task** tab, in the **Clipboard** section, click **Paste** or; • Right-click the ID number and choose **Paste** or; • Press **Ctrl+V.**
Adjust column width or row height	1. Place the mouse pointer over the column head divider or row divider. 2. Double-click to adjust automatically, or drag the divider.
Insert a task	1. Select the task below the row where you want to insert the new task. 2. Press **Insert.**
Delete a task	1. Select the entire task by clicking on the ID number for the task. 2. Press **Delete.**
Undo a mistake	• On the Quick Access toolbar, click **Undo** or; • Press **Ctrl+Z.**

Procedure Reference: Display a Summary Task Manually

To display a summary task manually:

1. On the **File** menu, click **Options** to view the **Project Options** dialog box.
2. On the **Advanced** page, in the **Display options for this project** section, check the **Show project summary task** check box.
3. If necessary, deselect the other check boxes except the **Show summary task** check box to display the summary task. Click **OK.** In the **Task Name** column, a new **Project summary task** appears with the task name in bold, and the task ID number as 0. The task is also converted to automatic task mode.
4. If necessary, select the **Project summary task** name and type the desired text.

ACTIVITY 2-3
Entering Tasks Manually into the Project Plan

Before You Begin:
The My Training Manual.mpp file is open.

Scenario:
During a weekly status meeting for the Training Manual project, the project team identified the high level phases of the project, as well as some of the key tasks needed for some of the phases. Because the project plan is in an early development phase, you decide to enter the information you have so far manually into the project plan file. This allows you to easily change any date and information later on.

---

1. Enter the summary tasks.

    a. In the **Entry** table, in the first row, in the **Task Name** column, type *Start Book*

    b. Press **Enter** so that the task name is entered into the **Entry** table and the active cell moves down to the next row.

    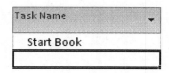

    c. Enter the other task names for the project: *Research Phase, Outline Phase, Development Phase, Test Phase, Review Phase, Print Phase,* and *Book Complete.*

1	🖋	Start Book
2	🖋	Research Phase
3	🖋	Outline Phase
4	🖋	Development Phase
5	🖋	Test Phase
6	🖋	Review Phase
7	🖋	Print Phase
8	🖋	Book Complete

---

2. Edit task 5.

    a.   In the **Entry** table, select task 5, **Test Phase.**

    b.   Click at the end of the text, then double-click the word **Test,** type *Edit* and press **Enter.**

3.   Display all the fields in the **Task Entry** table.

    a.   Position the mouse pointer on the divide bar between the **Task Entry** table and the **Gantt Chart.** Notice that the mouse pointer changes to a horizontal double-headed arrow.

    b.   Drag the mouse pointer approximately 3–inches to the right until the **Resource Names** column is visible in the **Entry** table.

4.   Enter the additional tasks, which will be the subtasks for task 2, Outline Phase.

    a.   In the **Entry** table, select task 3, **Outline Phase.**

    b.   Click the **Task** tab and then click **Task** to insert a new task above the selected row.

    c.   In the new task field, type *Interview Subject Matter Experts* and press **Enter.**

    d.   Position the mouse pointer on the column divider between the **Task Name** and the **Duration** columns and when the mouse pointer changes to a horizontal double-headed arrow, double-click to increase the width of the column.

    e.   Enter the other subtasks: *Investigate the Software* and *Search the Web.*

5.   Relocate task 3 to task 5.

    a.   Click the ID number for task 3, **Interview Subject Matter Experts,** to select the entire task.

 To move the entire task, be certain to select the ID number.

    b.   On the **Task** tab, in the **Clipboard** section, click **Cut.**

    c.   Click the ID number for task 5 and click **Paste.**

    d.   Click task 6 to view the relocated task clearly.

6.   Display the project summary task.

a. From the **File** menu, choose **Options** to display the **Project Options** dialog box.

b. In the left pane, click **Advanced.**

c. Scroll down to the **Display options for this project** section and check the **Show project summary task** check box.

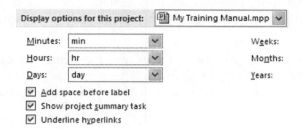

d. Click **OK** to display the project summary task.

e. Observe that in the **Task Name** column, the project summary task with the name **My Training Manual** appears in bold and the task ID number appears as **0.**

f. Notice that the duration for the project has been updated. Place the mouse pointer over the task mode for the project summary task and notice that it is converted to auto-scheduled mode, then hover over one of the other tasks and notice that the mode has not changed and remains in manual mode.

g. Save the file.

TOPIC D
Enter the Task Duration Estimates

Up to this point, you have created an activity plan that contains a simple list of tasks. Without knowing the duration of the tasks, it would be difficult to plan your project. In this topic, you will enter the task duration estimates.

For Project to accurately schedule the tasks in your project plan, you must enter the estimated duration for each task. Without duration, your project plan would be nothing more than a to-do list. With duration, it becomes more complete and the tasks can be linked more accurately within the project.

Duration

Definition:

Duration is the time interval between the start and end time of a task. In automatic task mode, Project assigns an estimate of a 1-day duration to each new task in the project plan. Day is the default parameter, and Project calculates 1 day as 8 hours, 1 week as 40 hours, and 1 month as 20 working days. There are other parameters such as minutes and hours to estimate the duration of the tasks. The duration settings can be altered using the **Project Options** dialog box on the **Schedule** page.

Example:

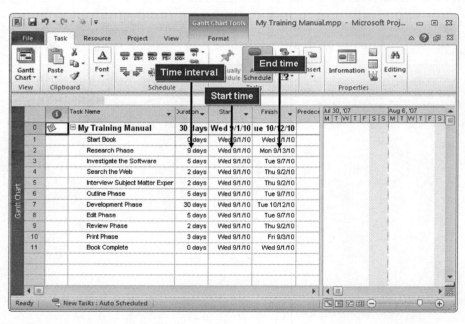

Figure 2-5: *Duration shown in Project.*

Duration Codes

The duration codes of the other parameters that can be used in a project are displayed in the table.

Duration	Displayed As
Minutes	m, min, minute.
Hours	h, hr, hour.
Days	d, dy, day.
Weeks	w, wk, week.
Elapsed Duration	emin, ehr, eday, ewk.
	Use elapsed duration when 24 hours by 7 days of continuous effort is needed. Usually used for unattended tasks such as allowing paint to dry or concrete to set.

The Duration Formula

When estimating the duration of tasks, it is helpful to seek the advice of people involved in the tasks. You can also use the formula $E = [O + P + (4 * M)]/6$ to create an estimated duration. In this formula:

- E = estimated duration.
- M = the most probable time.
- O = the most optimistic time (5% probability).
- P = the most pessimistic time (5% probability).

For example, if the optimistic duration is 2 weeks (w), the pessimistic duration is 10 weeks, and the most likely duration is 3 weeks, then the estimated duration is [2w + 10w + (4*3w)]/6 = 4 weeks.

Units

Definition:

A *unit* is the representation of the percentage of a resource's time assigned to a task. The default percentage is 100. However, if a resource would work only half the time on a task, you can set that resource's assignment units to 50 percent.

Example:

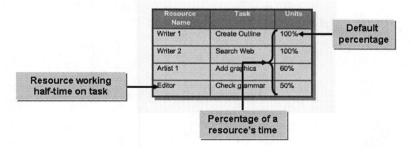

Figure 2-6: Units shown in Project.

Work

Definition:

Work is the amount of person-hours needed to complete each resource's assignment. The total work for a task is the sum of the work of all its assignments. The formula for calculating work is Work = Duration * Units. The total amount of time spent by the resource for its assigned tasks varies based on the nature of the task and the efficiency of the resource.

Example:

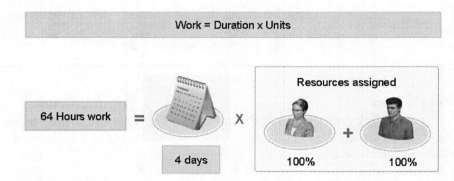

Figure 2-7: Calculating work.

Milestones

Definition:

A *milestone* is a task that acts as a reference point, which marks a major event in a project and is used to monitor the project's progress. As a general rule, you use milestones to mark the beginning and end of your project, the end of a major phase, or for a task for which the duration is unknown or out of your control. In the **Gantt Chart,** milestones are displayed with the symbol of a black diamond. Any task with zero duration is automatically displayed as a milestone. You can also mark any other task of any duration as a milestone by checking the **Mark task as milestone** check box available on the **Advanced** tab of the **Summary Task Information** dialog box.

Example:

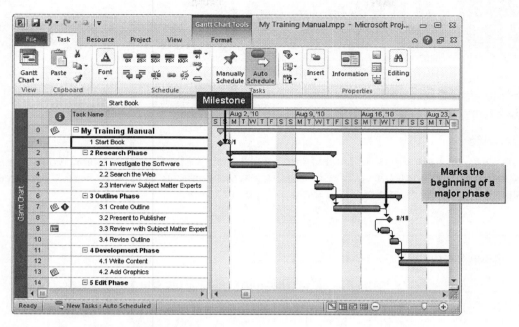

Figure 2-8: A milestone shown in Project.

How to Enter the Task Duration Estimates

Procedure Reference: Enter the Task Duration Estimates

To enter the task duration estimates in your project plan:

1. Open the project plan in the **Gantt Chart** view.

2. In the **Task Entry** table, select the **Duration** field for the task for which you wish to enter the duration.

3. Enter the duration for the tasks.

   - Type the desired number and press **Enter** or;
   - Click the arrows to the left of the text box.

4. If necessary, customize the duration.

   a. From the **File** menu, choose **Options** to display the **Project Options** dialog box.

   b. In the left pane, select **Schedule.**

   c. In the **Scheduling options for this project** section, select the **Duration is entered in** option list to customize the desired duration unit for the project tasks.

ACTIVITY 2-4
Entering the Task Duration Estimates

Before You Begin:

The My Training Manual.mpp file is open.

Scenario:

Now that you have the tasks entered into your Training Manual project plan, you must enter the estimated duration for each task. This step will be crucial to acquire needed resources when the schedule is approved by the development team.

1. Enter the duration for tasks 1 and 2.

    a. In the **Entry** table, select the **Duration** field for the **Start Book** task.

    b. In the first row, in the **Duration** field, click and type *0* and then press **Enter** to display the duration for the **Start Book** task in the **Gantt Chart**.

    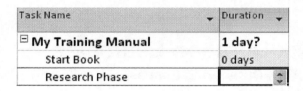

Task Name	Duration
⊟ **My Training Manual**	**1 day?**
Start Book	0 days
Research Phase	

    c. Observe that the **Gantt Chart** displays the diamond symbol against the **Start Book** task.

    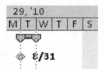

    d. In the second row, in the **Duration** column, type *9* and press **Enter** to display the duration of the **Research Phase** task.

2. **What screen changes occurred as a result of entering the task duration?**

    a) The summary task start and finish dates reflect the task duration.

    b) The active cell is automatically shifted to the next row.

    c) The length of the taskbar in the Gantt Chart increases to represent the duration.

    d) A Calendar icon is displayed in the indicators column of the selected task.

3. Enter the task duration for the remaining tasks.

    a. In the third row, in the **Duration** column, type *5* and press **Enter** to display the duration of the **Investigate the Software** task.

b.   Enter the duration for the rest of the tasks as *2, 2, 5, 30, 5, 2, 3,* and *0* days.

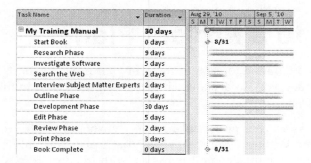

Task Name	Duration	Aug 29, '10 S M T W T F S	Sep 5, '10 S M T W
⊟ **My Training Manual**	**30 days**		
Start Book	0 days	◇ 8/31	
Research Phase	9 days		
Investigate Software	5 days		
Search the Web	2 days		
Interview Subject Matter Experts	2 days		
Outline Phase	5 days		
Development Phase	30 days		
Edit Phase	5 days		
Review Phase	2 days		
Print Phase	3 days		
Book Complete	0 days	◇ 8/31	

c.   Save the file.

TOPIC E
Add Resources to a Project Plan

So far, you created tasks and assigned duration to each of them in your project plan. Now, you need to determine who will perform the work to accomplish these assigned tasks. In this topic, you will add resources to a project plan.

If you plan to assign resources to tasks in your project plan, then you should be able to add the correct resources within your plan. Without resources, your project plan is simply a timeline of related tasks that theoretically will accomplish a goal. With the resources added, you can ensure that the project tasks get applied and that the work necessary to complete the project will get done.

Resources

Definition:

Resources are the people, equipment, material, and other miscellaneous items used to complete project tasks. Once assigned to project tasks, resources determine the duration and the cost details for each task.

Example:

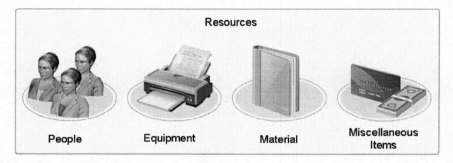

Figure 2-9: *Project resources.*

Types of Resources

Project classifies resources into different types.

Type	Description
Work resources	People or equipment. Example of work resources include the following:
	• Marjorie Westfall–An individual person.
	• Writer 1–A generic resource.
	• Editors–A group.
	• High-speed printer—A piece of equipment.

Type	Description
Material resources	Supplies or other consumable items used to complete tasks in a project. Examples of material resources include the following: ● Paper ● Ink ● Toner ● Raw material used for the manufacture of a product.
Cost resources	Miscellaneous expenses that vary from task to task and do not change by the amount of work performed on the task. Examples of cost resources include the following: ● Airfare ● Lodging
Budget resources	Project-level work, material, and cost resources. These capture the maximum capacity for a project to consume money, work, or material units. These resources can be applied only at the project level by assigning them to the project summary task.

Resource Sheet Fields

Information about resources can be maintained in a resource list, which can be created using the **Resource Sheet.**

Column Name	Description
ID	Contains an identifier number that Project automatically assigns to each resource.
Indicators	Displays icons that contain information about the resource.
Resource Name	Contains the name of the resource.
Type	Contains the resource type—**work, material,** or **cost.**
Material Label	Specifies the unit of measurement for a material resource. For example, steel can be measured in tons.
Initials	Specifies the resource name's abbreviation.
Group	Contains the name of the group that the resource belongs to—for example, external or internal resources.
Max. Units	Describes the percentage of work a resource can do when assigned to a task.
Std. Rate	Specifies the rate paid to the resource for regular and nonovertime work.
Ovt. Rate	Specifies the rate paid to the resource for overtime work.
Cost/Use	Specifies the cost that is accrued each time a resource is used.
Accrue At	Displays choices based on which costs, whether regular or overtime, will be calculated for a resource. This is either at the start or end of a task, or as a task is completed (prorated).
Base Calendar	Displays the calendar that is in use.
Code	Contains extra information about a resource.

The Resource Information Dialog Box

The **Resource Information** dialog box is used to enter, edit, and review information for selected resources in a project. The **Costs** tab displays options to enter, review, or change the cost information about the resource. On the **Notes** tab, you can enter or review the detailed notes about a specific resource. The **Custom Fields** tab allows you to enter and edit values for the resource's custom fields, if any.

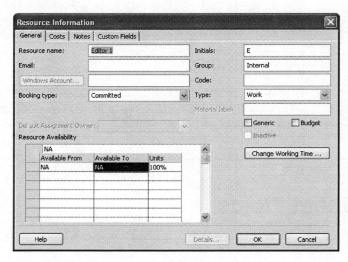

Figure 2-10: *Resource information.*

How to Add Resources to a Project Plan

Procedure Reference: Enter Resources in the Resource Sheet

To enter resources in the **Resource Sheet**:

1. Open the project plan.
2. On the **View** tab, click **Resource Sheet** to display the **Resource Sheet** view.
3. In the **Resource Entry** table, in the desired row, in the **Resource Name** field, type the resource name.
4. Press **Tab** to enter the resource and move to the **Type** field of the selected resource.
5. In the **Type** field, from the drop-down list, select the desired resource type and press **Tab** to move to the **Material Label** field.
6. If the resource is a material resource, in the **Material Label** field, enter the unit of measurement and press **Tab** to move to the **Initials** field.
7. Enter the **Initials** of the resource.
   - In the **Initials** field, accept the default initials by pressing **Tab.**
   - Type the desired initials and press **Tab.**
8. If necessary, if you wish to categorize the resources by group, in the **Group** field, type the group name and press **Tab** to move to the **Max. Units** field.

9. Enter the maximum units that a resource can work on.
    - In the **Max. Units** field, type the desired **Unit** or;
    - In the **Max. Units** field, use the arrows to select the desired unit.

10. If necessary, make entries to the other fields.

Procedure Reference: Enter Resources by Using the Resource Information Dialog Box

To enter the resources by using the **Resource Information** dialog box:

1. Open the desired project file and on the Ribbon, click the **Resource** tab.
2. In the **Properties** section, click **Information.**
3. On the **General** tab, enter the resource details and click **OK.**

Procedure Reference: Enter a Budget Resource in the Resource Sheet

To enter a budget resource in the **Resource Sheet:**

1. Display the **Resource Sheet** view.
2. In the **Resource Sheet,** enter all the necessary details about the resource.
3. If the resource is a budget resource, change the resource type.
    a. Display the **Resource Information** dialog box.
    b. On the **General** tab, check the **Budget** check box.
    c. Click **OK.**

Procedure Reference: Sort Resources in the Resource Sheet

To sort the resources displayed in the **Resource Sheet:**

1. Display the **Resource Sheet** view.
2. On the Ribbon, on the **View** tab, click the **Sort** drop-down arrow to display the **Sort** options.
3. Set your sort criteria for sorting the resources.
    - From the **Sort** submenu, choose **by Cost, by Name,** or **by ID** to sort the resources by cost, name, or by their ID.
    - Choose **Sort by** and in the **Sort** dialog box, set your sort criteria.

 If you check the **Permanently renumber resources** check box in the **Sort** dialog box, your resources will not return to their original numbered order.

ACTIVITY 2-5
Entering Resources by Using the Resource Sheet

Before You Begin:

The My Training Manual.mpp file is open.

Scenario:

After getting initial approval from the project stakeholders, resources are assigned to complete the tasks in your project. You are also provided with an approved budget for travel and other miscellaneous items needed for your project. Now that you have the resource information you need, you can enter the information properly into your project plan.

1. Enter the resources with their associated data.

    a. On the Ribbon, click the **View** tab.

    b. In the **Resource Views** section, click **Resource Sheet.**

    c. In the **Resource Entry** table, in the first row, in the **Resource Name** field, type **Writer 1** and press **Tab** to enter the resource name and move to the **Type** column of the selected resource.

    d. Observe that in the **Type** field, **Work** is selected and press **Tab** three times.

    e. In the first row, in the **Group** field, type **Internal** and press **Enter.**

	❶	Resource Name ▼	Type ▼	Material ▼	Initials ▼	Group ▼
1		Writer 1	Work		W	Internal

    f. In the **Resource Entry** table, enter the following information:

    *   **Resource Name: *Editor 1***
    *   **Type: *Work***
    *   **Group: *Internal***
    *   **Resource Name: *Project Manager 1***
    *   **Type: *Work***
    *   **Group: *Internal***
    *   **Resource Name: *Publisher***
    *   **Type: *Work***
    *   **Group: *Internal***

	❶	Resource Name ▼	Type ▼	Material ▼	Initials ▼	Group ▼
1		Writer 1	Work		W	Internal
2		Editor 1	Work		E	Internal
3		Project Manager 1	Work		P	Internal
4		Publisher	Work		P	Internal

2. Enter the rest of the resources with their associated data.

a. In the **Resource Entry** table, in the fifth row, in the **Resource Name** field, type *Subject Matter Expert* and press **Tab** four times.

b. In the fifth row, in the **Group** field, type *External* and press **Enter**.

c. In the sixth row, in the **Resource Name** field, type *Travel Expenses* and press **Tab**.

d. In the **Type** field, from the drop-down list, select **Cost** and press **Tab** three times.

e. In the sixth row, in the **Group** field, type *Internal* and press **Enter**.

f. In the seventh row, in the **Resource Name** field, type *Glossy Paper* and press **Tab**.

g. In the **Type** field, from the drop-down list, select **Material** and press **Tab**.

h. In the **Material Label** field, type *reams* and press **Tab** twice.

i. In the seventh row, in the **Group** field, type *External* and press **Enter**.

ℹ	Resource Name	Type	Material	Initials	Group
	Writer 1	Work		W	Internal
	Editor 1	Work		E	Internal
	Project Manager 1	Work		P	Internal
	Publisher	Work		P	Internal
	Subject Matter Expert	Work		S	External
	Travel Expenses	Cost		T	Internal
	Glossy Paper	Material	reams	G	External

3. Enter the budget resources.

a. In the eighth row, in the **Resource Name** field, type *Budget - Miscellaneous* and press **Tab**.

b. In the **Type** field, from the drop-down list, select **Cost** and press **Tab** three times.

c. In the eighth row, in the **Group** field, type *Internal* and press **Enter**.

d. In the **Resource Entry** table, select the eighth row.

e. On the Ribbon, click the **Resource** tab, and then click **Information** to launch the **Resource Information** dialog box.

f. On the **General** tab, check the **Budget** check box for the **Budget - Miscellaneous** resource.

g. Click **OK** to close the **Resource Information** dialog box.

h. In the **Resource Entry** table, in rows 9 and 10, enter the following budget resource information:

- **Resource Name:** *Budget - Labor*

- **Type:** *Work*
- **Group:** *Internal*
- **Resource Name:** *Budget - Material*
- **Type:** *Material*
- **Material Label:** *reams*
- **Group:** *Internal*

	ⓘ	Resource Name	▼	Type	▼	Material	▼	Initials	▼	Group	▼
1		Writer 1		Work				W		Internal	
2		Editor 1		Work				E		Internal	
3		Project Manager 1		Work				P		Internal	
4		Publisher		Work				P		Internal	
5		Subject Matter Expert		Work				S		External	
6		Travel Expenses		Cost				T		Internal	
7		Glossy Paper		Material		reams		G		External	
8		Budget - Miscellaneous		Cost				B		Internal	
9		Budget - Labor		Work				B		Internal	
10		Budget - Material		Material		reams		B		Internal	

i.   In the **Project Information** dialog box for both budget resources in rows 9 and 10, select the **Budget** option.

j.   Save and close the file.

Lesson 2 Follow-up

In this lesson, you created a project plan and assigned a project calendar to it. You also entered the tasks and their duration into the project plan. Entering this information accurately into your plan is the first step in ensuring that your project finishes on time, within budget, and within scope.

1. **In your job role, what types of tasks do you think you will use?**

2. **In your job role, when do you think milestones will be helpful?**

3 Managing Tasks in a Project Plan

Lesson Time: 1 hour(s), 30 minutes

Lesson Objectives:

In this lesson, you will manage tasks by organizing tasks and setting task relationships.

You will:

- Outline tasks in a project plan file.
- Link dependent tasks.
- Apply a constraint and deadline to a task.
- Add notes to a task.
- Add a recurring task.

Introduction

You now have a project plan that contains a complete list of project tasks and their duration, as well as the resources needed for the project. For Project to create a realistic schedule for these tasks, you will need to create relationships between the various tasks. In this lesson, you will manage your project plan by organizing tasks into more manageable pieces and forming relationships between them.

Managing all the tasks in a project plan file can be overwhelming, especially for large projects that involve many tasks. Project helps you manage these tasks by organizing them in a structure that shows how some tasks fit within broader groupings and how the tasks relate to one another. Properly managing the tasks in your plan allows you to make a well-organized project structure that can be edited and updated quickly.

TOPIC A
Outline Tasks

Up to this point, you entered your tasks along with their estimated duration in your project plan. Now, you need to differentiate between the various tasks in the project plan by breaking them down into manageable chunks. In this topic, you will outline tasks by converting them to summary tasks or subtasks.

As a project manager, you know that not all tasks are on the same level. Some tasks stand alone, while others comprise various other tasks. For example, you may have a summary task that requires many subtasks to complete it. By displaying the many levels of tasks in an organized manner, you can easily identify the hierarchical relationship between the summary task and the subtasks.

Work Breakdown Structures

Definition:

A *work breakdown structure* is a logical hierarchy of tasks in a project; it is represented by alphanumeric codes that identify the unique place of each task in the structure. Beginning with the project goal or objective, the project's work is progressively broken down until it reaches a level where you can estimate the duration of the lowest-level subtasks. The work breakdown structure can be drawn as a graphic that is displayed much like an organization chart with finite components, or it can be drawn as a simple outline.

Example:

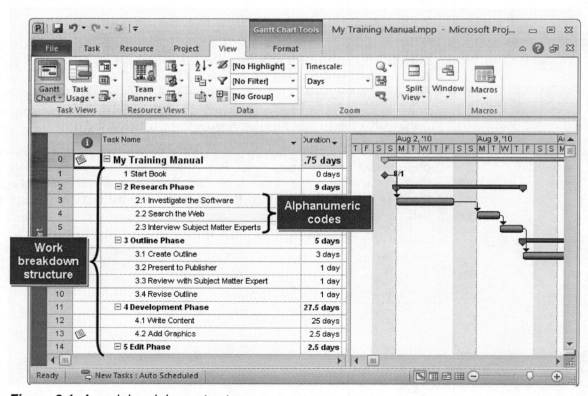

Figure 3-1: A work breakdown structure.

Outlining

Definition:

Outlining allows you to use the Gantt chart to organize the tasks in your plan into summary tasks and subtasks. Once you set tasks to subtasks and summary tasks, outlining assigns outline numbers that indicate the place of a task assignment in the project outline hierarchy. A task with an outline level of 1 is at the highest level in the outline, with no summary tasks above it. The number of outline levels you can set is unlimited for a task.

Example:

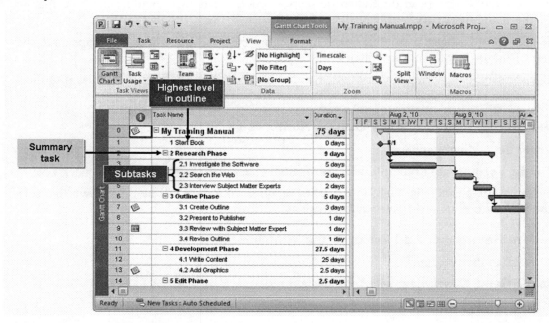

Figure 3-2: A sample outline.

Summary Task and Subtask Relationships

Schedule and cost information from subtasks are accumulated at the summary task level. The start date of a summary task is determined by the earliest start date of any of its subtasks. To display or hide the subtasks in your project plan, use the summary task's outline symbols, the plus (+) and minus (-) icons, which appear to the left of the task name.

How to Outline Tasks

Procedure Reference: Outline Tasks

To outline tasks in a project plan:

1. In the **Gantt Chart** view, in the **Task Name** column, select a task or group of tasks.
2. Outline the tasks as a subtask or summary task.
   - On the **Task** tab, in the **Schedule** section, click **Indent** to indent the task, making it a subtask.
   - On the **Task** tab, in the **Schedule** section, click **Outdent** to outdent the task, making it a summary task.
3. If necessary, collapse a summary task by clicking the (-) minus icon that appears to the left of the task you want to collapse.
4. If necessary, expand a summary task, by clicking the (+) plus icon that appears to the left of the task name.

Procedure Reference: Display Outline Numbers

To display the outline numbers:

1. On the **Format** tab, in the **Show/Hide** section, check the **Outline Number** check box.
2. If necessary, on the **View** tab, in the **Data** section, from the **Outline** drop-down list, select the desired outline level you want to display.

Procedure Reference: Add Tasks to the Timeline

To add tasks to the timeline:

1. In the **Gantt Chart** view, select the desired task.
2. Right-click the task and choose **Add to Timeline.**
3. Verify that the timeline is displayed with the correct task information.

ACTIVITY 3-1
Outlining Tasks in a Project Plan

Data Files:

C:\084602Data\Managing Tasks\Training Manual.mpp

Scenario:

While preparing the project plan for Our Global Company's new training manual project, you recognize that the tasks must be grouped properly to display the correct workflow for the project. Once you have outlined the tasks, you must verify the hierarchy and start building the project timeline to present at the monthly project managers' meeting.

---

1. Open the Training Manual.mpp file.

    a. On the Ribbon, choose **File→Open.**

    b. Navigate to C:\084602Data\ and double-click the **Managing Tasks** folder.

    c. In the file list area, select **Training Manual.mpp** and click **Open.**

---

2. Designate tasks as subtasks.

    a. In the **Gantt Chart** view, in the **Task Name** column, click task 3, hold down **Shift,** and click task 5.

    b. On the **Task** tab, in the **Schedule** section, click the **Indent** button.

---

3. Indent the remaining subtasks in the project plan.

    a. In the **Gantt Chart** view, in the **Task Name** column, select tasks 7, 8, and 9.

    b. On the **Task** tab, click the **Indent** button.

    c.   Indent the remaining tasks under **Development Phase, Edit Phase, Review Phase** and **Print Phase.**

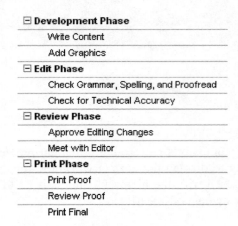

4.   Display the outline numbers in your project plan to show the hierarchy of tasks.

    a.   Click the **Format** tab, and in the **Show/Hide** section, check the **Outline Number** check box.

    b.   Click below task 23 to verify that the outline numbers for each of the tasks is displayed in the project plan.

5.   Add the project summary task to the timeline.

    a.   Select the **Training Manual** project summary task in the Gantt chart.

    b.   Right-click and choose **Add to Timeline.**

    c.   Verify that the timeline now displays the project summary task with the start and finish dates.

    d.   Save the file as *My Training Manual.mpp*

TOPIC B

Link Dependent Tasks

With your tasks organized as summary tasks and subtasks, your project plan looks more manageable and readable. You are now ready to form dependency relationships between the various tasks. In this topic, you will link dependent tasks in a project.

Creating relationships among tasks is the key factor in creating a realistic schedule that can be used to get actual work done on time. In order for Project to determine a project timeline or schedule, you must create relationships, or link necessary tasks.

Task Dependency Types

A task relationship or a dependency occurs when the starting time of a particular task, called the *successor*, is dependent on whether another task, called the *predecessor*, is starting or is completed. There are four kinds of dependencies.

Link Type	Description
Finish-to-Start (FS)	Task B cannot start until Task A is completed. For example, if you have two tasks, Lay Foundation and Pour Concrete, the Pour Concrete task cannot begin until the Lay Foundation task is completed. This link type is the default type assigned to new tasks in Project.
Start-to-Start (SS)	Task B cannot start until Task A starts. The dependent task can begin anytime after the task that it depends on begins. The SS link type does not require both tasks to begin simultaneously. For example, if you have two tasks, Pour Concrete and Level Concrete, the Level Concrete task cannot begin until the Pour Concrete task begins.
Finish-to-Finish (FF)	Task B cannot finish until Task A finishes. The dependent task can be completed anytime after the task that it depends on is completed. The FF link type does not require that both tasks be completed simultaneously. For example, if you have two tasks, Painting and Interior Designing, the Interior Designing task may start before or after the Painting task, but cannot finish until after the Painting task is completed.
Start-to-Finish (SF)	Task B cannot finish until task A starts. The dependent task can be completed anytime after the task it depends on begins. The SF link type does not require that the dependent task be completed concurrent with the beginning of the task on which it depends. For example, computer consultants must start installing software before they can finish testing computers.

The Lag Time

Definition:

Lag time is a delay between two dependent tasks. In a project plan, a lag time adds waiting time after a task is completed. Lag time is set between a maximum of two tasks and it must be set after a dependency is created between those tasks. Lag time can be entered either as a duration or as a percentage of the duration of the predecessor task. Lag time is always entered as a positive value.

Example:

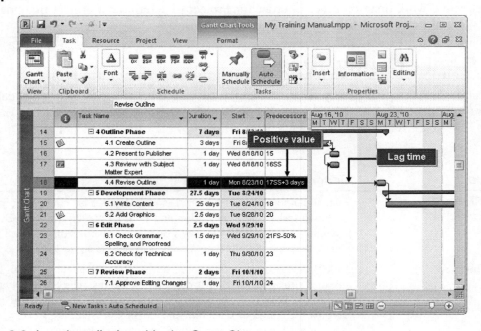

Figure 3-3: Lag time displayed in the Gantt Chart.

The Lead Time

Definition:

Lead time is the overlap between two tasks that are linked by a dependency. In a project, lead time is set for a task that can start when its predecessor task is partially finished. It is entered either as a duration or as a percentage of the duration of the predecessor task. Lead time can be set between a maximum of two tasks and it must be set after a dependency is created between those tasks. Lead time is always entered as a negative value.

Example:

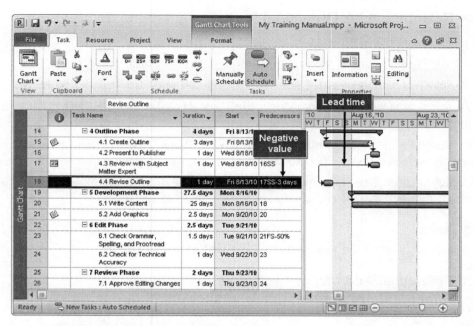

Figure 3-4: Lead time displayed in the Gantt Chart.

> The project management profession clearly distinguishes between the terms lag and lead, and they are functionally different. However, the Microsoft Project interface does not separate them in the project plan. Instead, Microsoft Project simply treats a lead as a lag time with a negative value.

The Task Information Dialog Box

The six tabs in the **Task Information** dialog box have various sections that you can use to enter, review, or change information about a selected task.

Tab	Used To
General	Enter duration of a task, track progress on a task by entering the percentage of completion, and enter the start and finish date for a task. It is also used to hide a taskbar and to roll up the subtasks to the summary taskbar.
Predecessors	Enter a predecessor, set the predecessor type, and enter the lag or lead time for a task.
Resources	Enter, review, or change resource assignments and assignment units for a selected task.
Advanced	Enter, review, or change additional task information for a task such as entering a deadline for task, change a constraint, and specify task type and task calendar.
Notes	Enter or review notes for a selected task.
Custom Fields	View and assign values to custom task fields and outline codes.

How to Link Dependent Tasks

Procedure Reference: Link Dependent Tasks

To link dependent tasks in a project:

1. In the **Task Name** column, select two or more dependent tasks to be linked.
   - To select nonadjacent tasks, hold down **Ctrl** and click the tasks to be linked.
   - To select adjacent tasks, hold down **Shift** and click the first and last tasks to be linked.
2. On the **Task** tab, in the **Schedule** section, click the **Link Tasks** button to create links between the selected tasks. Each successor task becomes dependent on the previous task.
3. If necessary, on the **Task** tab, click the **Unlink tasks** button to unlink the tasks. This will remove all the predecessor and successor links related to the task.

Unlinking Tasks

To unlink a task is to select the task and click the **Unlink tasks** button.

Procedure Reference: Add Lag or Lead Time

To add lag or lead time to a task:

1. Double-click the successor task for which you want to add lag or lead time.
2. In the **Task Information** dialog box, select the **Predecessors** tab.
3. In the **Lag** column, type the lead or lag time, either as a duration or as a percentage of the duration of the predecessor task.
   - To set the lag time, in the **Lag** column, enter either a positive number or a positive percentage value.
   - To set the lead time, in the **Lag** column, enter either a negative number or a negative percentage value.
4. Click **OK** and press **Enter.**

Procedure Reference: Change Task Predecessors

To change task predecessors:

1. In the **Task Name** column, double-click the task for which you need to change the predecessor.
2. In the **Task Information** dialog box, select the **Predecessors** tab.
3. Set a different task predecessor.
   - In the **Task Name** column, delete the predecessor displayed and enter a new predecessor or;
   - In the **Task Name** column, click the displayed predecessor to enable the predecessor drop-down arrow, and from the drop-down list, select the desired predecessor.
4. Click **OK.**

Procedure Reference: Modify Task Relationship Types

To modify task relationship types:

1. In the **Task Name** column, double-click the task for which you need to modify task relationship types.
2. In the **Task Information** dialog box, select the **Predecessor** tab.

3. In the **Type** column, click on the displayed type to enable the type drop-down arrow, and from the drop-down list that is displayed, select the desired type.

4. Click **OK.**

5. If necessary, on the **Task** tab, in the **Editing** section, click the **Scroll to Task** button to display it.

ACTIVITY 3-2
Linking Tasks in a Project Plan

Before You Begin:

The My Training Manual.mpp file is open.

Scenario:

Now that you have outlined your tasks, you want to form relationships between the various dependent tasks. You realize that you need to create a project timeline and also want a systematic succession of the tasks, **Interview Subject Matter Experts, Investigate the Software,** and **Search the Web.** You need to set dependencies between **Start Book** and **Interview Subject Matter Experts** and form a relationship between all the milestones and subtasks in the project.

1. Form a link between the adjacent tasks.

    a. In the **Task Name** column, select tasks 3, 4, and 5.

    b. Verify that the Gantt bars of the tasks are currently unlinked. On the **Task** tab, in the **Schedule** section, click the **Link Tasks** button.

    c. In the **Gantt Chart,** verify that the Gantt bars of the selected tasks are now linked.

2. Form a link between the nonadjacent tasks.

    a. In the **Task Name** column, select task 1, hold down **Ctrl,** and select task 3.

    b. On the **Task** tab, in the **Schedule** section, click the **Link Tasks** button.

    c. In the **Gantt Chart,** verify that the Gantt bars of the selected tasks are linked.

3. Link the remaining subtasks.

    a. Select tasks 5, 7, 8, and 9 and click the **Link Tasks** button to link the tasks.

    b. Link the tasks 9, 11, and 12; 12, 14, and 15; 15, 17, and 18; 18, 20, 21, and 22; 22 and 23 to complete the file.

    c. Save the file.

ACTIVITY 3-3
Modifying a Task Relationship Type

Before You Begin:

1. Drag the divide bar to the right until the **Predecessors** column is visible.

2. The My Training Manual.mpp file is open.

Scenario:

In your project plan, you realize that a task to review the outline with the subject matter expert is missing and needs to be added. You also know that this new task cannot start until its predecessor, task 8, starts. You need to update the project plan to reflect these changes.

---

1. Add a subtask to the **Outline Phase** summary task.

   a. Select task 9, **Revise Outline,** and press **Insert** to insert a new task in the row above.

   b. In the inserted row, in the **Task Name** column, type *Review with Subject Matter Expert* and press **Tab.**

   c. Type *1 day* and press **Enter.**

⊟ 3 Outline Phase	4 days	Fri 8/13/10
3.1 Create Outline	3 days	Fri 8/13/10
3.2 Present to Publisher	1 day	Wed 8/18/10
3.3 Review with Subject Matter Expert	1 day	Wed 8/18/10
3.4 Revise Outline	1 day	Fri 8/13/10

---

2. Change the task relationship type for the task **Review with Subject Matter Expert** to start-to-start.

   a. Double-click task 9, **Review with Subject Matter Expert,** to display the **Task Information** dialog box and select the **Predecessors** tab.

   b. Observe that the current predecessor is **Present to Publisher** and the relationship type is **Finish-to-Start (FS).** Click in the first cell of the **Type** column for the task **Present to Publisher.**

   c. From the **Type** drop-down list, select **Start-to-Start (SS)** and click **OK.**

   d. In the **Gantt Chart,** scroll to the right and view the screentips for tasks 8 and 9 to verify that they both start on the same day and then save the file.

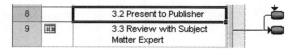

ACTIVITY 3-4
Adding Lead Time to a Task

Before You Begin:
The My Training Manual.mpp file is open.

Scenario:
As a project manager, you always need to look for ways to save time and money. As the editor can begin editing the manual before all the graphics are added, you decide to set a lead time to the task **Check Grammar, Spelling, and Proofread.**

---

1. Set 50 percent lead time for task 15.

    a. Double-click task 15, **Check Grammar, Spelling, and Proofread.**

    b. In the **Lag** column of the **Add Graphics** task, observe that **0d** is displayed, indicating that the lag time is set to zero days by default.

    c. In the **Lag** field, click and type **-50%** and then press **Enter.**

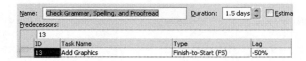

    d. Click **OK.**

---

2. Verify the lead time for task 15.

    a. If necessary, click and drag the divide bar until you view the **Predecessors** column.

    b. Select the **Predecessors** column of task 15.

    c. In the **Gantt Chart** view, scroll to the right to view the Gantt bars of the selected task.

    d. Verify that the **Predecessors** column displays the lead time, and the Gantt bars for tasks 13 and 15 overlap reflecting the new relationship with -50% as the lead time.

    e. Save the file.

TOPIC C
Set Task Constraints and Deadlines

In the previous topic, you formed links between tasks in your project plan, which in turn, schedules the start and finish dates for each project task. Having managed projects, you know how likely it is that other factors, such as personnel availability, will affect the actual start or finish dates of tasks. In this topic, you will set a constraint and a deadline to tasks to account for these factors.

Suppose you have a computer consultant who must install software for your project and is not available until after a specific date. This task will be a constraint for other dependent tasks to be completed or started at their scheduled time. In such a situation, you may need to add deadlines to specific tasks before the software install, or just set task constraints so that the project schedule is recalculated based on the constraint.

Task Constraints

Definition:

Constraints are conditions or limitations placed on the start or finish date of a task in a project plan. Task constraints are applied only in automatic task mode and may affect the overall project schedule and duration. When you set a project using a start date, by default, all tasks are scheduled to start with an **As Soon As Possible** constraint. If the project is set using a finish date, tasks are scheduled to start with an **As Late As Possible** constraint. When a constraint is set for a task, an icon is displayed in the **Indicators** column to the left of the task. Project then recalculates the scheduled tasks that are affected by the constraint, unless you are scheduling from the project finish date and applying an **As Late As Possible** constraint.

Example:

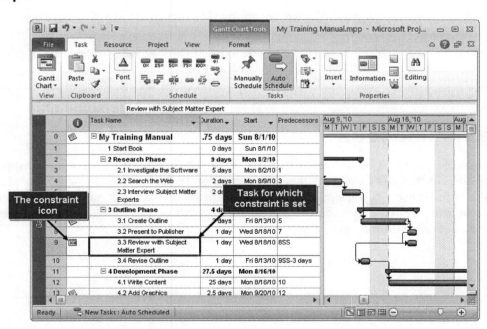

Figure 3-5: A task constraint.

Task Indicator Icons

Project uses indicator icons to represent information about the state of a task, a resource, or an assignment. These indicators are displayed in the **Indicators** column. The **Indicators** column is located to the right of the ID number and will display various graphical icons. To view a screentip containing the important information associated with a task, a resource, or an assignment, place the mouse pointer over the icon.

Task Constraint Types

There are different types of constraints with various degrees of flexibility.

Constraint Type	Description
As Soon As Possible	The task is scheduled to start as soon as possible, based on other constraints and relationships in the project. This is the default constraint in a project scheduled from the start date. It is the most flexible constraint.
As Late As Possible	The task is scheduled to finish as late as possible, based on other constraints and relationships in the project. This is the default constraint in a project scheduled from the finish date. It is a flexible constraint.
Start No Earlier Than	The task must be scheduled to start on the specified date or later. It is a less flexible constraint.
Start No Later Than	The task must be scheduled to start on the specified date or sooner. It is a less flexible constraint.
Finish No Earlier Than	The task must be scheduled to finish on the specified date or later. It is a less flexible constraint.
Finish No Later Than	The task must be scheduled to finish on the specified date or sooner. It is a less flexible constraint.
Must Start On	The task must be scheduled to start on the specified date. It is one of the least flexible constraints.
Must Finish On	The task must be scheduled to finish on the specified date. It is one of the least flexible constraints.

The Task Inspector

The *Task Inspector* pane can be displayed from the **Task** tab, in the **Tasks** section. It displays to the left of the **Gantt Chart** and provides information on factors affecting a specific task. This pane can also be used to track schedule changes. If the selected task has a constraint, the **Task Inspector** pane displays the type of constraint that is currently placed on the task, including the date associated with the constraint.

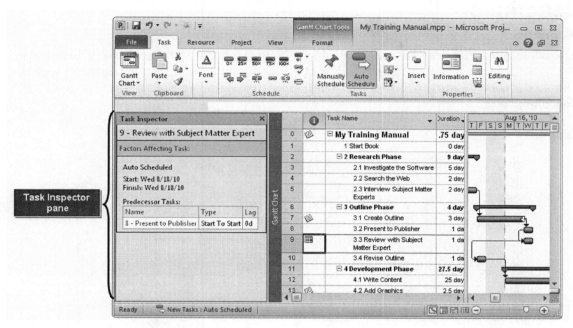

Figure 3-6: *The Task Inspector pane.*

The Task Inspector Tools

There are a number of tools that the **Task Inspector** uses to help resolve scheduling issues.

Tool	Description
Warnings	The **Task Inspector** pane will display warnings and suggested changes when there are conflicting tasks, leveling issues, or specific task constraints affecting your schedule.
Overallocations	The **Task Inspector** pane will identify resource overallocations for a selected task and provide suggestions to resolve any issue.
Calendar	When a calendar is assigned to a project and the working time is affecting the task schedule, the **Task Inspector** pane will display the calendar's name so that you can resolve any issue.
Auto and Manually Scheduled tasks	The **Task Inspector** pane will display the current mode of a task. You can easily switch the mode of a task at any time.

Deadlines

Definition:

A *deadline* is a target date that indicates when you want a task to be completed. If the deadline date passes and the task is incomplete, Project displays a downward pointing arrow as an indicator in the **Gantt Chart.** Unlike a constraint, a deadline does not directly affect project scheduling dates.

Example:

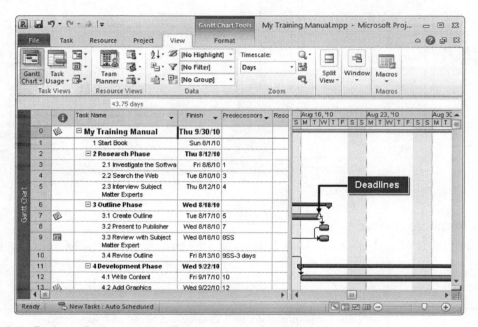

Figure 3-7: *Project displays a deadline as a downward pointing arrow.*

How to Set Constraints and Deadlines on Tasks

Procedure Reference: Apply a Constraint or Deadline to a Task

To apply a constraint or deadline to a task:

1. Double-click the task for which you need to apply a constraint.
2. In the **Task Information** dialog box, select the **Advanced** tab.
3. In the **Constraint Task** section, click the **Constraint type** drop-down arrow to display the drop-down list and select the desired type of constraint to set a constraint.
4. In the **Constraint Task** section, click the **Deadline** drop-down arrow and from the calendar that is displayed, select the finish date for the task to set a deadline.
5. Click the **Constraint date** drop-down arrow to display the calendar and from the calendar that is displayed, select the desired date.
6. Click **OK.**

Date Constraints

If tasks change, causing you to miss a deadline, a constraint causes a warning message box to be displayed. You can also change the way Project honors task constraints. If you want Project to note the conflict, without considering it when creating the project schedule, choose **File→ Options,** select the **Schedule** page, and in the **Scheduling options for this project** section, uncheck the **Tasks will always honor their constraint dates** check box.

ACTIVITY 3-5
Setting a Constraint and a Deadline

Before You Begin:
The My Training Manual.mpp file is open.

Scenario:
As per your project schedule, the writer must meet with the subject matter expert to review the outline at the earliest opportunity after the outline is completed. Recently, you received the information that the subject matter expert will not be available as scheduled. Therefore, the task has to be postponed. No matter what else changes in the schedule, the review cannot begin before 8/20/10. So, you need to keep track of this inflexible constraint. However, because so many other parts of the project depend on the outline being completed in a timely fashion, you cannot let this delay in the start of the Subject Matter Expert review cause a delay in the completion of the outline. So, you decide to set an explicit deadline of 8/17/10 to ensure that the outline is completed before the next relevant task.

1. Set the date constraint for the **Review with Subject Matter Expert** task.

   a. Double-click task 9, **Review with Subject Matter Expert**.

   b. In the **Task Information** dialog box, select the **Advanced** tab.

   c. In the **Constraint task** section, from the **Constraint type** drop-down list, select **Start No Earlier Than.**

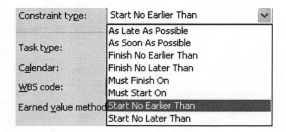

   d. From the **Constraint date** drop-down calendar, select the constraint date as **August 20, 2010.**

   e. Click **OK.**

2. Verify the constraint for task 9.

   a. Notice that all the dependent tasks' start and finish dates are highlighted blue and have been adjusted to accommodate the added constraint to the schedule.

   b. Place the mouse pointer over the constraint icon, in the **Indicators** column to view constraint details.

   c. On the **Task** tab, in the **Tasks** section, click the **Inspect** button to display the **Task Inspector** pane.

    d.   Observe that the **Task Inspector** pane on the left displays the **Constraint type** as **Start No Earlier Than** and **Constraint date** as **Fri 8/20/10.**

    e.   Close the **Task Inspector** pane.

3.   Set a deadline for the **Create Outline** task.

    a.   Double-click task 7, **Create Outline.**

    b.   On the **Advanced** tab, in the **Constraint task** section, in the **Deadline** drop-down calendar, set the date to **August 17, 2010.**

    c.   Click **OK** to set the deadline date.

    d.   Observe that the start and finish dates for the task and all the dependent tasks have not changed.

4.   Check whether the deadline is displayed in the **Gantt Chart.**

    a.   In the **Gantt Chart,** on the Gantt bar for task 7, place the mouse pointer over the downward pointing white arrow and view the screentip for the task displaying the deadline.

    b.   Save the file.

TOPIC D
Add Notes to a Task

After organizing tasks and establishing task relationships, you have more or less captured all the data related to tasks in your project plan. However, you might need to flag some information relevant to a task that may be of use later, or function as a reminder note. In this topic, you will add such information, in the form of notes, to a task.

In general, keeping notes is a best practice, when you need to refer to something that was mentioned in a business meeting or interview. The same concept applies when you are working in Project. For example, adding a note that reminds you to provide a customer with a physical CD at the end of a development task will ensure that you do not miss the actual deliverable. Microsoft Project will help you create and track task notes during the project.

Task Notes

Definition:

Task notes are additional or supporting information that is added to a task. You can add notes to record specifications, customer requirements, quality measures, or any general information related to a task. Project also offers the flexibility to attach related documents, including Microsoft Word or Microsoft Excel files, or to create hyperlinks to supporting information.

Example:

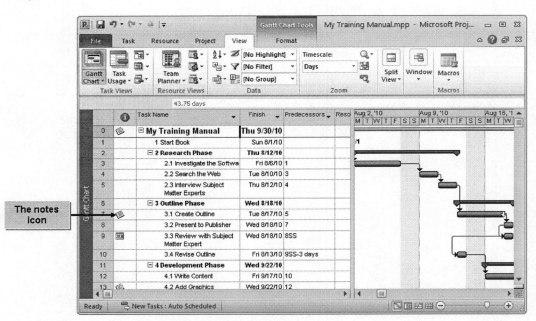

Figure 3-8: A project with notes added to tasks.

How to Add Notes to a Task

Procedure Reference: Add Notes to a Task

To add notes to a task:

1. Select the desired task or resource to which you want to add a note.
2. On the Ribbon, choose the desired note.
   - On the **Task** tab, in the **Properties** section, choose **Task Notes** to add a task note or;
   - On the **Resource** tab, in the **Properties** section, choose **Notes** to add a resource note.
3. Click in the **Notes** text area to enter the desired note.
4. Click **OK** to insert the desired notes.

Procedure Reference: Format Notes

To format notes in a project:

1. Select the desired sheet view.
2. Double-click the task with the note you want to format.
3. On the **Notes** tab, in the **Notes** text area, select the note in the text area.
4. In the **Notes** section, click a button to apply the desired formatting to the selected note.
   - Click the **Format Font** button to display the **Font** dialog box and choose the desired option to change the font.
   - Click the **Align Left** button to align notes on the left side.
   - Click **Center** to align notes to the center.
   - Click the **Align Right** button to align notes to the right.
   - Click the **Bulleted List** button to display notes as a bulleted list.
   - Click the **Insert Object** button to display the **Insert Object** dialog box and choose the desired option to insert objects to notes.
5. Click **OK** to format the note.

ACTIVITY 3-6
Adding Notes to a Task

Before You Begin:

The My Training Manual.mpp file is open.

Scenario:

As the project manager of the training manual project, you need to keep track of all the project-related information that is crucial to completing tasks, but is not required to be entered as individual tasks in the plan. You will add supplemental notes to some of the subtasks in your project, to make sure that specific handoff information is included in the project plan.

1. Add notes to the **Create Outline, Add Graphics,** and **Print Proof** tasks.

   a. In the **Task Name** column, double-click task 7 to display the **Task Information** dialog box.

   b. Select the **Notes** tab.

   c. In the **Notes** text area, type *Send Outline.doc to the HR department.*

   d. Click **OK** to insert the note.

   e. Double-click task 13 and in the **Notes** text area, type *Based on the storyboard, insert appropriate graphics for the content.*

   f. Click **OK** to insert the note.

   g. Double-click task 21 and in the **Notes** text area, type *Provide a hard copy proof to the project manager.*

   h. Click **OK** to insert the note.

2. Display the screentip for the **Notes** indicator for the **Create Outline** task.

   a. Click task 7.

   b. In the **Indicators** column for task 7, place the mouse pointer over the notes indicator icon, 📝 to view the notes message for the task.

   c. Save the file.

TOPIC E
Add a Recurring Task

So far, you have added tasks that occur only once throughout a project's life cycle. But there are some tasks, such as status meetings, which occur repeatedly at some particular time interval in the project plan. These tasks can occur multiple times throughout a project's life cycle. In this topic, you will add a recurring task.

Project related meetings and check points can occur weekly, monthly, or at regular intervals throughout a project. Project allows you to designate these types of recurring events so that you do not have to enter them as separate tasks multiple times. This can be very useful when organizing recurring project tasks and can also save you time and energy, as well as help eliminate errors.

Recurring Tasks

Definition:

A *recurring task* is a task that occurs repeatedly at regular intervals during the course of a project. Rather than entering these tasks multiple times, they can be entered once as a recurring task using the **Recurring Task Information** dialog box. A recurring task appears as a summary task with multiple subtasks that represent each occurrence of the task. They are identified by the recurring task indicator icon, which appears to the left of the task in the **Indicators** column. A recurring task can be inserted in the project at any point in a project cycle.

Example:

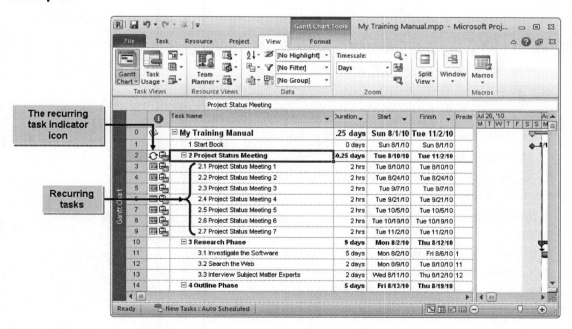

Figure 3-9: *A recurring task.*

The Recurring Task Information Dialog Box

The **Recurring Task Information** dialog box helps you add a recurring task, or review details about an existing recurring task. The recurring task names are entered in the **Task Name** text box and the recurrence pattern for the task is set by selecting the desired options under the **Recurrence pattern** section, which sets the frequency of the task occurrence and the desired day. This dialog box also allows you to set the start date and the end date for a project under the **Range of recurrence** section and helps assign the desired calendar for scheduling the project from the **Calendar** drop-down list.

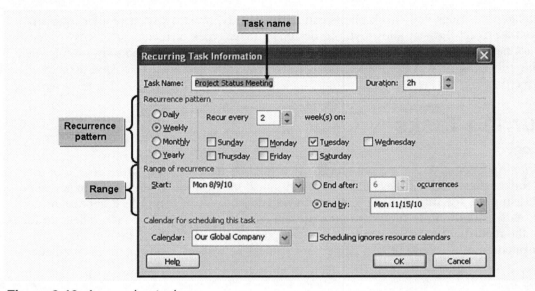

Figure 3-10: A recurring task.

How to Add a Recurring Task

Procedure Reference: Add a Recurring Task

To add a recurring task:

1. Choose **View→Gantt Chart.**
2. In the **Task Name** column, select a row to insert the recurring task.
3. On the **Task** tab, in the **Insert** section, choose **Task→Recurring Task.**
4. In the **Recurring Task Information** dialog box, in the **Task Name** text box, type a name for the recurring task.
5. In the **Durations** text box, double-click and type the duration for which the task will occur.
6. In the **Recurrence pattern** section, check the desired options to set the frequency of occurrence and the day on which the task should recur.

7. In the **Range of recurrence** section, set the start and end dates of the recurring task.

    • Click the **Start** drop-down arrow and from the calendar that is displayed, select the start date for the recurring task.

    • Check the **End after** check box to end the recurring task after a specific number of occurrences and specify the desired number in the **occurrences** spin box.

    • Check the **End by** check box, and click the **End by** drop-down arrow, and from the calendar that is displayed, select the end date to end the recurring task on that particular date.

8. In the **Calendar for scheduling this task** section, from the **Calendar** drop-down list, select the desired type of calendar.

9. Click **OK** to insert the recurring task.

ACTIVITY 3-7
Adding a Recurring Task

Before You Begin:

The My Training Manual.mpp file is open.

Scenario:

You want to know the status of a project at regular intervals. So, you want to conduct a bi-weekly status meeting with the team on every other Tuesday for 2 hours. The meetings will start on August 09, 2010 and will end by November 15, 2010 based on the assigned Our Global Company calendar. Now that you have the above specifications, you are ready to incorporate the events into the project plan.

1. Add a recurring task.

   a. In the **Task Name** column, select task 2.

   b. On the **Task** tab, in the **Insert** section, choose **Task→Recurring Task.**

   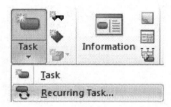

   c. In the **Recurring Task Information** dialog box, in the **Task Name** text box, type *Project Status Meeting*

   d. In the **Duration** text box, double-click and type *2 hrs*

   e. In the **Recurrence pattern** section, verify that the **Weekly** option is selected.

   f. In the **Recur every** text box, double-click and type *2* to set the task occurrence interval as biweekly.

   g. Check the **Tuesday** check box to specify the day of the week on which the task should be scheduled.

   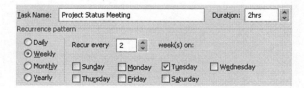

   h. In the **Range of recurrence** section, click the **Start** drop-down arrow.

   i. In the calendar that is displayed, set the start date to **August 09, 2010.**

   j. Click the **End by** drop-down arrow.

k. In the calendar that is displayed, set the end date as **November 15, 2010.**

l. In the **Calendar for scheduling this task** section, from the **Calendar** drop-down list, select **Our Global Company.**

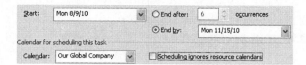

m. Click **OK.**

2. Display the entered subtasks.

a. Notice the bars added to the Gantt for each meeting instance. Expand the **Project Status Meeting** task to view the subtasks added with duration, start, and finish information.

b. In the **Indicators** column, place the mouse pointer over the recurring task indicator to view the information provided by the screentip.

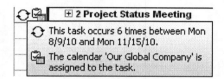

c. Save and close the file.

Lesson 3 Follow-up

In this lesson, you managed tasks by organizing them and setting task relationships. This will help you manage the project timeline for each task, and will ultimately ensure that the project is completed as scheduled.

1. **When might you set a deadline in your project plan?**

2. **What type of task relationships might you use? If you can, give an example of something you have experienced in your personal or professional life that falls into one of the task relationship categories.**

4 | Managing Resources in a Project Plan

Lesson Time: 1 hour(s), 30 minutes

Lesson Objectives:

In this lesson, you will manage resources for a project.

You will:

- Create a resource calendar.
- Assign resources to tasks.
- Enter associated costs for resources in the project plan file.
- Resolve resource conflicts.

Introduction

So far, you have set up a basic project plan, added tasks and resources, and organized the tasks in your project plan. Now, in order for your project to get underway, you will need to assign resources to perform the necessary work to complete these tasks. In this lesson, you will manage the resources used in your project.

If you create a to-do list for a project without identifying who will perform the necessary work to complete the items, it is likely that the items on the list will never be addressed. Similarly, if you want to use Project to track the amount of work done, or the amount of materials used in completing a project, you will have to use resources in your project plan file. Managing resources also enables the calculation of a more accurate schedule of the duration of each task.

TOPIC A
Create a Resource Calendar

In the previous lesson, you managed the tasks within your project plan. Now, you will cycle back to focus on the project resources you added along with the tasks at the time that you first set up the plan. A typical first step in resource management is to create resource calendars that can be applied to your project, because you will need these in place to properly schedule any resource with nonstandard work hours. In this topic, you will create a resource calendar.

For Project to correctly schedule resources to work on tasks, you must create and assign a resource calendar for those resources that do not work for the hours specified in the project calendar. Perhaps you have a resource who works part-time. If you neglect to create a different calendar for this employee, your schedule will be incorrect because it will allocate the resource for a full 8-hour day, instead of the 4-hour day that he actually works. Being able to separate resource schedules from the project calendar is a big step toward proper resource and project management.

The Resource Information Dialog Box

The **Resource Information** dialog box is used to configure individual resources. It can be used to create a resource calendar, adjust availability settings, edit working time, add contact information, and manage resource costs.

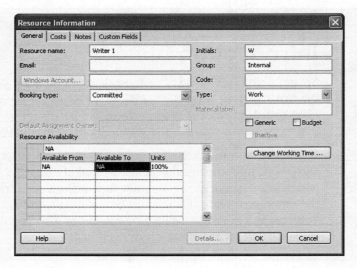

Figure 4-1: *Resource information.*

How to Create a Resource Calendar

Procedure Reference: Create a Resource Calendar

To create a resource calendar:

1. Display the **Resource Sheet** view.
2. Double-click the resource for which you need to create a resource calendar.
3. In the **Resource Information** dialog box, on the **General** tab, click **Change Working Time.**
4. In the **Change Working Time** dialog box, make the necessary working time edits to the resource calendar information.
5. Click **OK** to save the changes.
6. In the **Resource Information** dialog box, click **OK.**

 You can also change the resource calendar information in the **Change Working Time** dialog box available on the **Project** tab.

ACTIVITY 4-1
Creating a Resource Calendar

Data Files:

C:\084602Data\Managing Resources\Training Manual.mpp

Scenario:

As the project manager for the OGC training manual development project, you have just been told that, as of today, the **Staff Assistant 2** resource is changing her employment status to part-time. To accommodate this change in your plan, you need to change her working hours. You know that the working hours are Monday to Friday, from 8:00 A.M.–12:00 P.M. Additionally, the resource is only available to work on the project from October 15, 2010 through November 30, 2010.

---

1. Display the **Change Working Time** dialog box for the resource, **Staff Assistant 2.**

    a. Open the C:\084602Data\Managing Resources\Training Manual.mpp file.

    b. In the Training Manual.mpp file, on the **View** tab, in the **Resource Views** section, click **Resource Sheet.**

    c. In the **Resource Name** column, double-click Resource 9, **Staff Assistant 2,** to display the **Resource Information** dialog box.

    d. On the **General** tab, click **Change Working Time** to display the **Change Working Time** dialog box.

---

2. Alter the calendar to reflect an 8:00 A.M.–12:00 P.M. work schedule, Monday through Friday.

    a. In the **Change Working Time** dialog box, in the **Click on a day to see its working times** calendar preview, scroll down to **October 2010** and select **15.**

    b. Select the **Work Weeks** tab.

    c. Verify that the **[Default]** working time row is selected and click **Details.**

    d. In the **Details for '[Default]'** dialog box, in the **Select day(s)** list box, notice that **Monday** is selected by default. Hold down **Shift** and then click **Friday** to select the **Monday** to **Friday** working week.

    e. Select the **Set day(s) to these specific working times** option to set the new timings for **Staff Assistant 2.**

f.   In the second row, select the **From** field and press **Delete** to delete the afternoon working hours from **1:00 PM** to **5:00 PM.**

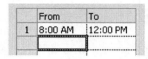

g.   To close the **Details for '[Default]'** dialog box, click **OK.**

h.   To close the **Change Working Time** dialog box, click **OK.**

---

3.   Change the availability of the **Staff Assistant 2** resource.

a.   In the **Resource Information** dialog box, in the **Resource Availability** section, in the first row, select the **Available From** field and type *10/15/2010*

b.   In the first row, in the **Available To** field, click and type *11/30/2010*

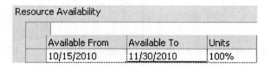

---

4.   Add a note to the **Staff Assistant 2** resource.

a.   In the **Resource Information** dialog box, select the **Notes** tab.

b.   In the **Notes** text box, click and type *Given enough notice, this resource can work afternoons, instead of mornings.*

c.   Click **OK** to add the note to the resource and to close the **Resource Information** dialog box.

d.   Save the file as *My Training Manual.mpp*

TOPIC B
Assign Resources to Tasks

In the previous topic, you created a calendar for a resource who works on a different schedule. With resources entered and resource calendars decided, you are ready for the next step in the creation of your project plan, which is to connect the resources with the appropriate tasks. In this topic, you will assign resources to the tasks in your project plan.

Imagine a project plan where none of the team members know what their responsibilities are. These projects, if they get off the ground at all, are chaotic and confusing, and will never be managed or governed correctly. To avoid this, you need to identify who is responsible for completing the tasks in your project plan and assign resources to these tasks. By assigning resources, you allow Project to accurately schedule tasks by using the resource calendars and assignment units information. Furthermore, you can then use Project to help you account for resource time and costs.

Part-Time Resources

A *part-time resource* is one that is scheduled either to work less than 40 hours in a work week, or who spends no more than 50 percent of their work time on a project. Normally, in a project, full-time resources are scheduled to work 40 hours and 100 percent of their calendar time on tasks. In Microsoft Project, this information is registered in the **Max. Units** field in various views. If you need to assign resources to work less than 100 percent of their time on a task, you can alter the information in this field by entering the correct percentage.

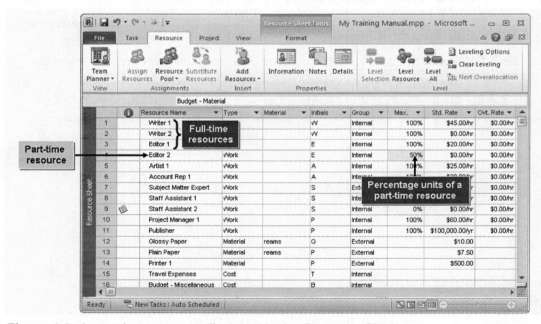

Figure 4-2: *A part-time resource displayed in the Resource Sheet.*

Effort-Driven Scheduling

Effort-driven scheduling is a method used to determine what happens to the duration or resource units for a task when you add or remove resources. When you assign resources to an effort-driven task, Project shortens the task duration and when you remove resources from a task, Project lengthens the task duration. It does not, however, change the total work for the task. Effort-driven scheduling is off by default in Project 2010.

Task Variables

You can control the way your task schedule is managed by setting any of the three variables—duration, work, or units—to unchangeable in scheduling calculations. Setting any of the three task variables as fixed provides an extra measure of control over the project schedule. Because the duration of each task is determined by the formula, `Duration = Work / Units`, you can choose that part of the equation that Project calculates by setting the **Task type.**

Task Types

To control a task variable, you can set any of the three task variables as fixed by using the **Task type** drop-down list.

Task Type	Description
Fixed Units	A task with a fixed unit value. This is the default **Task type** in Project. Assigning additional resources to a task reduces the task's duration. For example, if one resource is assigned to complete the task of stuffing envelopes, adding another resource will shorten this task's duration. When effort-driven scheduling is turned on, then adding resources shortens the duration for that task. However, if effort-driven is turned off, then adding resources increases the total amount of work, but the units and the duration remain the same.
Fixed Duration	A task with a fixed value of duration. Any change made to the work, or to the assigned resources, does not impact the task's duration. Assigning additional resources to this task type decreases the individual unit values for resources. For example, if a delivery is made from one site to another and only one truck is necessary to complete the task, assigning additional resources to the task does not decrease the task's duration. When effort-driven scheduling is turned on, adding resources decreases the units for each resource. When effort-driven scheduling is turned off, then adding resources increases the total work and keeps the units and duration the same.
Fixed Work	A task in which the amount of work to be completed is fixed. If changes are made to the task's duration, or to the number of assigned resources, there is no impact on work. Assigning additional resources shortens the duration of the task for this task type. When you set the task type as **Fixed work,** effort-driven scheduling is automatically turned on and you do not have the option to turn it off.

The Split View

When you want to display two views simultaneously, you can use the *split view* section of the **View** tab to quickly add either the **Details** or the **Timeline** view to your current display. When you add the **Timeline** view, it appears beneath the Ribbon in the top pane and shows the entire project's timeline. The **Details** view appears in the bottom pane of the view and shows detailed information about the data selected in the top pane. The default contents of the **Timeline** and **Details** views will change depending on the contents of your current display, but you can select a different form to display in either view. For example, the **Detail** pane will typically display the **Resource Form, Resource Graph,** or **Task Form.**

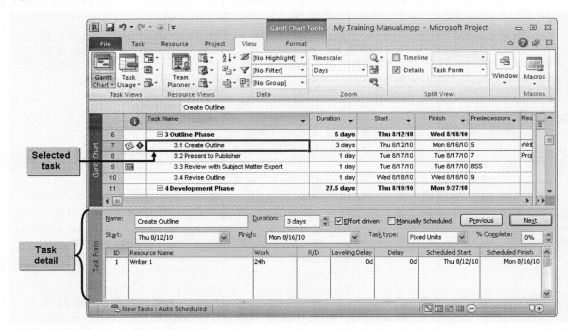

Figure 4-3: *The Details split view.*

The Task Form

The **Task Form** is a Project view that displays a form for entering and editing information about a task. When used in a split view, the **Task Form** can be very helpful, allowing you to display, enter, or edit the detailed information for a selected task. The **Previous** and **Next** buttons can be used to move forward and backward through a task list.

How to Assign Resources to Tasks

Procedure Reference: Assign Resources to Tasks by Using the Assign Resources Dialog Box

To assign resources to tasks by using the **Assign Resources** dialog box:

1. Display the **Gantt Chart** view.
2. In the **Task Entry** table, in the desired row, in the **Task Name** field, select the desired task for which you want to assign a resource to.
3. Display the **Assign Resources** dialog box.
   - On the **Resource** tab, in the **Assignments** section, click **Assign Resources** or;
   - On the keyboard, press **Alt+F10.**
4. In the **Resources** section, in the **Resource Name** field, select the resource or the resources that you want to assign.

 To select multiple resources, press **Ctrl.**

5. Click **Assign.** A check mark will appear next to the resource name.
6. If necessary, assign resources for other tasks within your project plan.
7. When finished, click **Close.**

 To remove an assigned resource, display the **Assign Resources** dialog box, select the resource to be removed, and click **Remove.**

Procedure Reference: Assign Resources by Using the Task Entry Table

To assign resources by using the **Task Entry** table:

1. Display the **Gantt Chart** view.
2. Drag the divide bar to the right so that the **Resource Names** column is displayed.
3. In the **Task Entry** table, in the desired row, in the **Resource Names** field, select the task that you want to assign a resource to.
4. From the required task's **Resource Names** drop-down list, check the desired resource's check box and press **Enter.**

Procedure Reference: Assign Resources by Using the Task Information Dialog Box

To assign resources by using the **Task Information** dialog box:

1. Display the **Gantt Chart** or the **Task Usage** view.
2. Select the desired task and display the **Task Information** dialog box.
3. Select the **Resources** tab.

4. In the **Resources** section, assign the desired resource to the task.

   - In the **Resource Name** column, select the desired cell and type the desired resource name or;

   - In the **Resource Name** column, from the desired cell's drop-down list, select the desired resource name.

5. Click **OK.**

 You can use the **Task Form** in the split view for this procedure by selecting the desired view on the **View** tab in the **Split View** section.

Procedure Reference: Assign Resources to Tasks by Using the Split View Task Form

To assign resources to tasks by using the **Split View Task Form:**

1. Select the appropriate primary view for your project.

2. On the **View** tab, in the **Split View** section, check the **Details** check box to add the **Details** view with the current view.

3. If the **Task Form** does not appear by default in the **Details** pane, select **Task Form** from the drop-down list in the **Split View** section.

4. In the **Task Form,** in the **Resource Name** column, assign the resources to the task.

5. If necessary, for a work resource, check the **Effort driven** check box to calculate the cost based on the effort and press **Enter.**

6. If necessary, click the **Previous** or **Next** button to navigate to other tasks and add resources to them.

Procedure Reference: Change a Task Type

To change the type of a task:

1. Display the **Gantt Chart** view.

2. Double-click the desired task to display the **Task Information** dialog box.

3. On the **Advanced** tab, from the **Task type** drop-down list, select the task type that you want to set and click **OK.**

 You can also change the type of a task by using the **Task type** drop-down list in the **Task Form.**

Procedure Reference: Change the Effort-Driven Scheduling for a Task

To change the effort-driven scheduling for a task:

1. Display the **Gantt Chart** view.

2. Double-click the desired task. In the **Task Information** dialog box, select the **Advanced** tab.

3. Check or uncheck the **Effort driven** check box and click **OK.**

ACTIVITY 4-2
Assigning Resources to a Task

Before You Begin:

The My Training Manual.mpp file is open.

Scenario:

After entering the tasks and the list of resources, you would like to link the resources with their designated tasks and make necessary changes to other tasks. Also, as the manager of your project, you have some tasks in the project schedule that you need to assign to yourself.

1. Display the split view with the **Gantt Chart** in the top pane.

    a. On the **View** tab, click **Gantt Chart.**

    b. Drag the divide bar to the far right of the screen so that all the fields in the **Task Entry** table are visible.

    c. On the **View** tab, in the **Split View** section, check **Details.**

    d. Verify that the **Task Form** is displayed in the **Details** pane.

2. Assign a resource to task 3.

    a. In the **Gantt Chart** view, select task 3, **Investigate the Software.**

    b. On the **Resource** tab, click **Assign Resources.**

    c. If necessary, drag the **Assign Resources** dialog box to the bottom-right corner of the window so that you can see all of the **Task Form** information.

    d. Scroll down, click **Writer 1** and then click **Assign.**

    e. Click **Close** to close the **Assign Resources** dialog box.

    f. Verify that in the **Task Entry** table, in the **Resource Names** field, **Writer 1** is listed for task 3, **Investigate the Software.**

3. Assign the **Writer 1** resource to tasks 4, 5, 7, and 8.

a. In the **Task Entry** table, select the **Resource Names** field for task 4, **Search the Web.**

b. In the **Resource Names** field, in the drop-down list, check **Writer 1** and press **Enter** to assign the resource to the task.

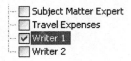

c. In the **Resource Names** field, from the drop-down list for task 5, **Interview Subject Matter Experts,** select **Writer 1** and press **Enter.**

d. In the **Task Form** view, click **Next** twice to switch to task 7, **Create Outline.**

e. In the **Task Form** view, in the first row, in the **Resource Name** field, from the drop-down list, select **Writer 1.**

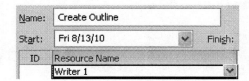

f. In the **Task Form** view, click **OK** to assign the resource to the task and click **Next** to move to task 8, **Present to Publisher.**

g. In the **Task Form** view, in the first row, in the **Resource Name** field, from the drop-down list, select **Writer 1** and click **OK** to assign the resource.

4. Reduce the duration of task 5 by changing the task to effort driven and assigning **Project Manager 1** as a second resource.

a. In the **Task Entry** table, select task 5, **Interview Subject Matter Experts.**

b. Observe that in the **Gantt Chart** view, the duration of the task is **2 days,** and in the **Task Form** view, the **Writer 1** resource is working 100% and works for 16 hours.

c. In the **Task Form,** check **Effort-Driven** to change the way Project calculates the task's duration.

d. In the **Task Form,** in the **Resource Names** column, click underneath the **Writer 1** resource and select **Project Manager 1** and then press **Enter.**

5. Verify the new duration, units, and work values for task 5.

a. Notice that in the **Gantt Chart** view, the duration of the task is reduced to one day, and in the **Task Form** view, both the **Writer 1** and **Project Manager 1** resources are working for 8 hours each as displayed in the **Work** column.

b. Notice that the task type is **Fixed Units.** Because the task type is fixed units and effort-driven scheduling is turned on, then, when the additional resource was assigned, Project recalculates the duration to one day, assumes both resources are working 100 percent of their time on this task, and splits the work hours between the two resources to 8 hours each.

6. Assign **Project Manager 1** as a second resource to the **Present to Publisher** task, without changing the duration of the task.

   a. In the **Task Entry** table, select task 8.

   b. In the **Task Form** view, verify that **Effort driven** is unchecked and that the task type is fixed units in order to keep the task's duration constant, independent of the number of assigned resources.

   c. In the **Task Form** view, click under the **Writer 1** resource and in the **Resource Name** drop-down list, scroll down and select **Project Manager 1.**

   d. In the **Task Form** view, click **OK.**

   e. If necessary, in the **Gantt Chart** view, widen the **Resource Names** column.

   f. Observe that the duration of task 8 remains the same, at **1 day**, because the task type is set to fixed units and effort-driven is turned off. The duration and units remain the same, but the amount of work is increased in this case. Both **Writer 1** and **Project Manager 1** will work for 8 hours.

7. Edit the resource **Project Manager 1** to work only part-time on task 8.

   a. In the **Task Form,** in the second row, click in the **Work** field and use the down-arrow button to set the work to **4h.**

   b. Click **OK.**

8. Add **Staff Assistant 1** as a second resource to task 4.

   a. In the **Task Entry** table, select task 4, **Search the Web.**

   b. On the **Resource** tab, click the **Assign Resources** button.

   c. Scroll down and select **Staff Assistant 1** and then click **Assign.**

   d. In the **Assign Resources** dialog box, click **Close.**

   e. Drag the divide bar approximately 3 inches to the left to view the **Gantt Chart.**

   f. In the **Gantt Chart** view, observe that for task 4, both **Writer 1** and **Staff Assistant 1** resources are assigned, and for task 5, both **Writer 1** and **Project Manager 1** resources are assigned.

   g. On the **View** tab, in the **Split View** section, uncheck **Details** and then save the file.

TOPIC C
Enter Costs for Resources

So far in this lesson, you assigned employee resources to the various tasks in your plan. After assigning the resources, you are ready to estimate the overall cost of the project and the cost of each of the resources. In this topic, you will enter the various costs for resources.

As a project manager, you are responsible for tracking and managing project costs. You cannot estimate the total project cost unless the cost details for individual resources are recorded. With the necessary information entered in the project plan, it is easy to calculate the total project cost and also identify the resources and tasks that involve huge costs. This is important if you have any hope of gleaning accurate financial information from your project plan.

Cost Options

You need to consider the different cost options when you enter costs for your project resources.

Cost Option	Description
Cost per use	This field is used when the cost of a work resource (people and equipment) has a set fee. The cost per use field in Project displays the cost that is accrued each time the resource is used. Work resources can have a cost per use value and an hourly rate applied.
Fixed cost accrual	This field is used when you are using fixed costs for a task. This field can be set to charge the fixed cost at the start, or end of a task, or can be set to prorate the cost across the duration of the task. The fixed cost is accrued based on the percent complete.
Budgeted costs	This field can be assigned to a project by configuring the budget work and budget cost values for the project summary task. The budget fields can be added to the **Gantt Chart** from the **Add New Column** drop-down list.

How to Enter Costs for Resources

Procedure Reference: Enter Costs for Work and Material Resources by Using the Resource Sheet

To enter costs for work and material resources by using the **Resource Sheet:**

1. Display the **Resource Sheet** view.
2. In the **Resource Name** column, select the desired resource.

 If the resource for which you would like to enter cost is not available, enter it as a new resource.

3. In the desired resource's row, in the **Std. Rate** field, type the cost associated with the resource.
4. If necessary, in the desired resource's row, in the **Ovt. Rate** field, type the overtime cost for the resource.

Procedure Reference: Enter Costs for Work and Material Resources by Using the Resource Information Dialog Box

To enter costs for work and material resources by using the **Resource Information** dialog box:

1. Display the **Resource Sheet** view.
2. Display the **Resource Information** dialog box.
3. Select the **Costs** tab.
4. In the **Cost rate tables** section, on the **A (Default)** tab, in the desired row, in the **Standard Rate** field, type the cost associated with the resource.
5. If necessary, in the desired row, in the **Overtime Rate** field, type the overtime rate of the resource.
6. If there is any change in the cost of the resources, enter the new cost value.
   - For a work resource, if the cost change comes into effect on another date, in the desired row, in the **Effective Date** field, enter the new date.
   - For a material resource, if the rate has increased by some value or percentage, in the next row, in the **Standard Rate** field, enter the value or percentage change.
7. Click **OK.**

Procedure Reference: Enter Costs for a Cost Resource

To enter costs for a cost resource:

1. Display the **Resource Sheet** view.
2. Enter the resource details, and from the **Type** drop-down list, select **Cost.**
3. Display the **Gantt Chart** view.
4. Assign the cost resource to the desired task.
5. Display the **Task Usage** view.
6. Select the cost resource assigned to the desired task and double-click to display the **Assignment Information** dialog box.
7. On the **General** tab, in the **Cost** text box, enter the cost for the resource.
8. Click **OK.**

9. If necessary, display the **Gantt Chart** view and widen the **Resource Names** column to view the amount entered for the cost resource.

 A single cost resource that is assigned to different tasks can have different cost values, for example, airfare for different trips.

Procedure Reference: Enter Values for Budget Resources

To enter values for budget resources:

1. In the **Resource Sheet** view, enter the budget resource.
2. Display the **Gantt Chart** view.
3. If necessary, display the project summary task.
4. In the project summary task, in the **Resource Names** column, assign the budget resource.
5. On the **View** tab, click **Resource Usage.**
6. In the **Resource Usage** view, in the **Add New** column, select **Budget Cost** and then select **Budget Work** to add both columns to the view.
7. In the **type of budget resource** column, in the project summary task available below the budget resource, enter the desired budget value.

ACTIVITY 4-3
Entering Costs for Resources

Before You Begin:
The My Training Manual.mpp file is open.

Scenario:
Once the resources have been assigned to the appropriate tasks in the project plan for the training manual development, you can add the correct costs for the necessary resources.

1. Enter the cost information for the work resources.

   a. Switch to the **Resource Sheet** view.

   b. In the sixth row, select the **Std. Rate** field of the **Account Rep 1** resource.

   c. Type *20/hr* and press **Enter.**

   d. In the **Resource Sheet** view, enter the following information:

   - **Writer 1-** *45/hr*
   - **Editor 1-** *20/hr*
   - **Artist 1-** *25/hr*
   - **Subject Matter Expert-** *100/hr*
   - **Staff Assistant 1-** *15/hr*
   - **Project Manager 1-** *60/hr*
   - **Publisher-** *100,000/yr*

Writer 1	Work	W	Internal	100%	$45.00/hr
Writer 2	Work	W	Internal	100%	$0.00/hr
Editor 1	Work	E	Internal	100%	$20.00/hr
Editor 2	Work	E	Internal	50%	$0.00/hr
Artist 1	Work	A	Internal	100%	$25.00/hr
Account Rep 1	Work	A	Internal	100%	$20.00/hr
Subject Matter Expert	Work	S	External	100%	$100.00/hr
Staff Assistant 1	Work	S	Internal	100%	$15.00/hr
Staff Assistant 2	Work	S	Internal	0%	$0.00/hr
Project Manager 1	Work	P	Internal	100%	$60.00/hr
Publisher	Work	P	Internal	100%	$100,000.00/yr

2. Enter the costs for the material resources.

   a. In the **Resource Sheet** view, in the 12th row, in the **Std. Rate** field of the **Glossy Paper** resource, type *10* and press **Enter.**

   b.   Enter the costs for the remaining material resources: *7.50* for **Plain Paper** and *500* for the **Printer 1** resources.

Glossy Paper	Material	reams	G	External		$10.00
Plain Paper	Material	reams	P	External		$7.50
Printer 1	Material		P	External		$500.00

3.   Enter the cost payable to the cost resource.

   a.   Display the **Gantt Chart** view.

   b.   If necessary, drag the divide bar to the far right of the application window. Also, widen the **Resource Names** column to display all the names properly.

   c.   In task 8, **Present to Publisher,** select the **Resource Names** field.

   d.   Click after **Project Manager 1,** insert a comma, then type *Travel Expenses* and press **Enter.**

   e.   If necessary, widen the **Resource Names** column.

   f.   On the **View** tab, click **Task Usage** to display the **Task Usage** view.

   g.   If necessary, widen the **Task Name** column.

   h.   In the **Task Name** column, below the **Present to Publisher** task, double-click the **Travel Expenses** resource to display the **Assignment Information** dialog box.

   i.   On the **General** tab, in the **Cost** text box, triple-click, type *250* and click **OK.**

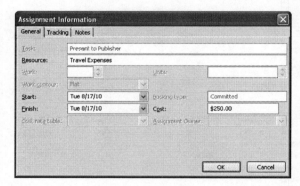

   j.   Switch to the **Gantt Chart** view and widen the **Resource Names** column to view the value entered for the **Travel Expenses** cost resource.

   k.   Save and close the file.

TOPIC D
Resolve Resource Conflicts

Now that you have entered all your resource information and assigned your resources, you might find that some of the resources are over scheduled and conflicts exist between the available resources and the tasks. In this topic, you will resolve resource conflicts.

For your project tasks to be accomplished on time, the assigned resources must perform the necessary work. In some cases, assigned resources can be inadvertently over-scheduled, perhaps by either working beyond their normal 40-hour work week, or working on multiple tasks simultaneously. Situations like these put the success of the project at risk. As a project manager, you might use creative solutions such as reassigning resources, hiring additional resources, requiring overtime work, or perhaps deciding to start the project earlier. How you decide to resolve the issue of overallocation will depend on factors such as cost, resource availability, and schedule flexibility, but whatever approach you take should be reflected in your project plan.

Resource Allocation

Resource allocation refers to the amount of time a resource is assigned to work on specific tasks and projects. Resources can be allocated to a number of tasks and projects at any given time and can be *overallocated* when the work time assigned to a resource is beyond its capacity. Overallocations can occur either because a resource is assigned to too many tasks, or because more resource units than available are assigned to a single task.

Resource Allocation Views

Project offers several views for displaying the resource allocation information. Within these views, overallocations are identified in various ways, depending on the view that you are looking at.

View	Description
Team Planner	The overallocated resource names will be displayed in red.
Resource Sheet	The allocated resources appear as red and are indicated by an exclamation point in the **Indicators** column.

View	Description
Resource Graph	The overallocated resources will be displayed in red and in the bar chart, red bars indicate that the resource has exceeded the maximum unit and working time that are available in the given time period. 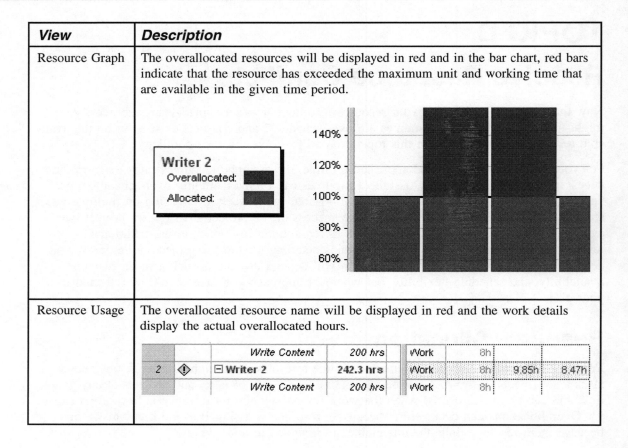
Resource Usage	The overallocated resource name will be displayed in red and the work details display the actual overallocated hours.

			Write Content	200 hrs	Work	8h		
2	◇	⊟ Writer 2		242.3 hrs	Work	8h	9.85h	8.47h
			Write Content	200 hrs	Work	8h		

Leveling

Once you have identified any overallocated resource in a project plan, you will need to determine the way in which you can correct the allocation. Microsoft Project offers a possible solution called *leveling,* which is the process of delaying or splitting tasks to resolve conflicts. Tasks are either split or delayed until the resources assigned are no longer overloaded. As a result, leveling can extend the project's finish date. It is important to note that leveling does not change resource assignments, nor does it add additional resources. By default, resources are not leveled automatically. By manually leveling overallocated resources, you can make leveling decisions based on other project factors such as lowest cost, earliest project finish date, or resource schedules.

Slack

When Project levels your overallocated resources, it determines the tasks that have to be split or delayed by looking at the task ID, available slack, task priority, task dependencies, task constraints, and scheduling dates. *Slack* is the amount of time a task can slip before it affects another task's dates or the project finish date.

Resource Leveling Options

The different sections in the **Resource Leveling** dialog box have options that help you in leveling the overallocated resources.

Section Name	Description
Leveling calculations	Allows you to specify whether the resources should be leveled automatically or manually upon the detection of an overallocated resource. Also, you can select a time period for the project; based on this time period, you can determine whether there are any overallocated resources.
Leveling range	Allows you to select an option based on which you can level the entire project or only those tasks falling under the specified time period.

Section Name	Description
Resolving overalloca-tions	Allows you to specify the order in which the overallocated tasks can be delayed or split. It also allows you to: ● Select **Level only within available slack** if you do not want Project to delay your project finish date (off by default). If you check this setting, you may still have overallocations in your project after leveling. ● Select **Leveling can adjust individual assignments on a task** if you want Project to level a resource independent of other resources working on the same task (on by default). ● Select **Leveling can create splits in remaining work** if you want Project to interrupt tasks by creating splits in the remaining work on tasks or resource assignments (on by default). ● Select **Level resources with the proposed booking type** if you want Project to include tasks using proposed and confirmed resources. Resolving overallocations Leveling order: [Priority, Standard ▾] ☐ Level only within available slack ☑ Leveling can adjust individual assignments on a task ☐ Leveling can create splits in remaining work ☐ Level resources with the proposed booking type ☑ Level manually scheduled tasks

How to Resolve Resource Conflicts

Procedure Reference: Resolve Resource Conflicts By Using Manual Leveling

To resolve resource conflicts by using manual leveling:

1. In the desired view, on the **Resource** tab, in the **Level** section, click **Leveling Options** to display the **Resource Leveling** dialog box.

 Before leveling, as a best practice, save the file with a different name, so that you can revert if you are not satisfied with the leveling results.

2. In the **Leveling calculations** section, verify that the **Manual** option is selected.
3. In the **Leveling range for <heading>** section, select the desired option for leveling the project.
   - Select **Level entire project** to level the entire project plan.
   - Select **Level** and include a **From** and **To** date range to level part of the plan.
4. In the **Resolving overallocations** section, select a leveling order to determine the task that is to be delayed or split in order to resolve resource overallocations.
5. In the **Resolving overallocations** section, check the desired check box for leveling and click **Level All.**

6. Review the changes in the **Leveling Gantt Chart** view, and if you are pleased with the results, save the file.

ACTIVITY 4-4
Resolving Resource Conflicts

Data Files:

C:\084602Data\Managing Resources\Training Manual Allocations.mpp

Scenario:

While you were out of the office for a couple of days, your colleague assigned the remaining resources to the tasks in the Training Manual project plan. You would like to view the data to ensure that the resources have been assigned to tasks correctly and that they are not burdened with too many tasks.

---

1. Display the resource graph information for **Writer 2** for the weeks between September 24, 2010 and October 1, 2010.

    a. Open the C:\084602Data\Managing Resources\Training Manual Allocations.mpp file.

    b. In the Training Manual Allocations.mpp file, in the **Resource Name** column, select **Writer 2.**

    c. On the **View** tab, in the **Resource Views** section, from the **Other Views** drop-down list, select the **Resource Graph** view.

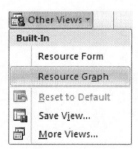

    d. In the right side of the graph, scroll to display the week of September 20, 2010.

e.   In the **Resource Graph** view, observe that the blue bars indicate that the **Writer 2** resource is working at 100 percent, while the red bars indicate that the resource is overallocated on the 23rd and 24th of September 2010.

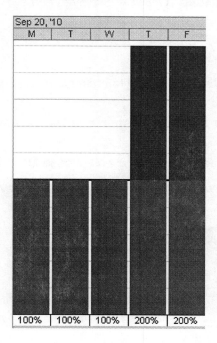

2.   Display the overallocated resources in the **Team Planner.**

   a.   On the **View** tab, click the **Team Planner** button.

   b.   In the **Resource Name** list, observe that the overallocated resources are red. In the right pane, scroll to view the tasks assigned to **Writer 2** and **Staff Assistant 2.**

   c.   Display the screentips for the tasks highlighted in red to view the specific task information. Notice that this view provides a **Task Path** at the bottom that allows you to see the flow of tasks related to this task.

   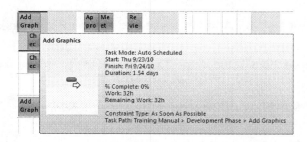

3.   Verify the project finish date before leveling the overallocated resources.

a. On the **Project** tab, click **Project Information** to display the **Project Information for 'Training Manual Allocations.mpp'** dialog box.

b. In the **Finish date** text box, observe that **Tues 10/4/10** is displayed and click **OK** to close the dialog box.

4. Resolve allocation issues for the **Writer 2** resource.

a. Save the file as ***My Training Manual Allocations.mpp*** to preserve a copy of the file prior to leveling.

b. In the **Resource Name** list, select **Writer 2.** On the **Resource** tab, in the **Level** section, click **Level Resource.**

c. On the **View** tab, click the **Other Views** drop-down menu and choose **More Views.**

d. In the **More Views** dialog box, in the **Views** list box, scroll up and select **Leveling Gantt.**

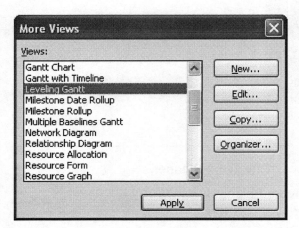

e. Click **Apply.**

f. In the **Leveling Gantt** view, on the right side, scroll to display the weeks between September 20, 2010 and October 4, 2010.

g. In the **Leveling Gantt** view, place the mouse pointer over the gray bar for task 15, **Check Grammar, Spelling, and Proofread.** Observe that the screentip displays the preleveled start and finish time along with the duration for the task.

h. Place the mouse pointer over the blue bar for task 13, **Add Graphics.** Observe that the screentip displays the actual start and finish dates along with its duration and a potential scheduling problem.

i. Right-click on the blue bar for task 13, **Add Graphics** and choose **Fix in Task Inspector.**

j. Observe the issues and suggestions listed in the **Task Inspector** pane and then click the **close** button.

k. Save the file as ***My Training Manual Allocations after leveling.mpp***

5. Resolve allocation issues for the **Staff Assistant 2** resource by reassigning the **Add Graphics** task to an available resource.

a. Switch to the **Team Planner** view. In the **Resource Name** list, double-click the **Staff Assistant 2** resource.

b. Observe that this resource is only available from 10/15/2010 to 11/30/2010. Click **OK.**

c. Display the screentip for the **Add Graphics** task in the right pane and notice that the start and finish dates for this task are scheduled after the **Staff Assistant 2** resource is available.

d. In the right pane, right-click the **Add Graphics** task and choose **Reassign To→Staff Assistant 1.**

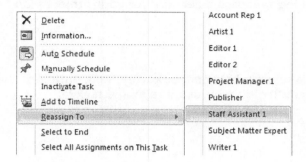

e. Save and close the file.

Lesson 4 Follow-up

In this lesson, you managed the resources in your project plan. Properly assigning and editing resource assignments is crucial to keeping an updated project plan. With this information captured correctly in your project plan, you can manage and track both the total work done and the resources used for completing the project.

1. **In your experience, how can using resource calendars for your project plan be beneficial?**

2. **How will understanding the relationship between task work, task duration, and task units help you when assigning multiple resources to a single task?**

5 | **Finalizing a Project Plan**

Lesson Time: 1 hour(s)

Lesson Objectives:

In this lesson, you will finalize a project plan.

You will:

- Shorten a project using the critical path.
- Set a project baseline.
- Print a project summary report.

Introduction

In the previous lesson, you worked with a project plan that includes tasks and assigned resources. With this data entered into the project plan, you can verify and manage the project finish date. Because this finish date may not always be acceptable, you need to verify the total project duration, as well as capture project plan information for future comparison. In this lesson, you will finalize the project plan.

There are many aspects of a project plan to manage when you are trying to finalize the plan. You must be able to determine whether the project finish date is acceptable or not, and how the plan will be presented and delivered to the necessary people. In order for you to control the schedule using Project, you must familiarize yourself with the techniques involved in finalizing a project plan.

TOPIC A
Shorten a Project Using the Critical Path

Now that you have a complete list of tasks with resources assigned, you are ready to make adjustments to the project as a whole. At this point, you will want to check your project finish date to determine whether it is acceptable. As a result, you may find that the schedule needs to be adjusted. In this topic, you will shorten the project using the critical path.

As a project manager, you will need to adjust a project's total duration at some point or the other. The idea is to get the job done in an acceptable time frame, within an agreed-upon budget, and to meet the project specifications. To reduce the total duration, you will need to know which tasks in the project plan actually affect the project's finish date. Your job, as a project manager, will include paying close attention to managing these tasks and making the needed adjustments to the project's duration.

Critical Paths

Definition:

A *critical path* is the series of tasks that determine the calculated finish date of a project. In a project, the critical path can show if the project will finish on time and also highlight the danger points. Tasks on the critical path are called *critical tasks*; if one or more of these critical tasks are delayed, the project will finish late. If a noncritical series of linked tasks slips its dates, this series of tasks may become the critical path. In complex or large projects, there can be more than one critical path or critical path section, and the critical path can change many times throughout a project's life cycle.

Example:

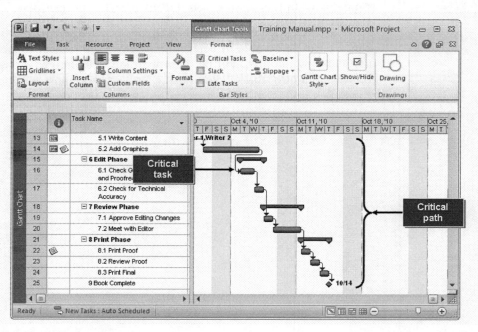

Figure 5-1: *A critical path.*

Schedule Warnings

Schedule warnings appear in Project when a change creates a potential scheduling conflict with a manually scheduled task's start date, finish date, or duration. The information with the potential problem is underlined with a red wavy line. You can then right-click the field to open the **Task Inspector** to read the scheduling warnings and possible solutions to improve the project.

Critical Path Views

You can view the critical path for a given plan in Project in a few different ways.

View	Description
Gantt Chart	In this view, you can display the critical path from the Ribbon, on the **Format** tab, in the **Bar Styles** section. You can choose to display the critical tasks, slack, and Late Tasks, as well as the available formatting options for the bars shown in the view. By default, the critical task bars are red in this view.
	The **Detail Gantt** view is similar to the **Gantt Chart**, except that it displays slack values to the right of the task bars. This view can be opened from the **More Views** dialog box.
Gantt Chart Wizard	In this view, you can use the options available to customize your **Gantt Chart.** The wizard can be used to display the critical path in the **Gantt Chart** view. The wizard has options to configure bar styles and layout options. You can re-configure any manually applied bar style by running the **Gantt Chart Wizard.**
Network Diagram	In this view, the critical tasks are colored red while the noncritical tasks are colored blue. This view allows you to see what tasks are critical to the project finish, along with the task information.

The Bar Styles Dialog Box

The **Bar Styles** dialog box is used to format the **Gantt Chart** bars. It is used to emphasize attributes, including critical tasks, milestones, summary tasks, and slacks. One set of style is associated with each chart-type view.

Slack

Definition:

Slack is the amount of time that a task can slip before it affects another task or the project's finish date. **Free Slack** is the amount of time a task can slip before it delays another task. **Total Slack** is the amount of time a task can slip before it delays the project finish date. If **Total Slack** is a negative number, it indicates the amount of time that must be saved so that the project finish date is not extended. Slack can be displayed by the **Gantt Chart** view and is represented by thin black bars that extend from a Gantt bar for a task.

Example:

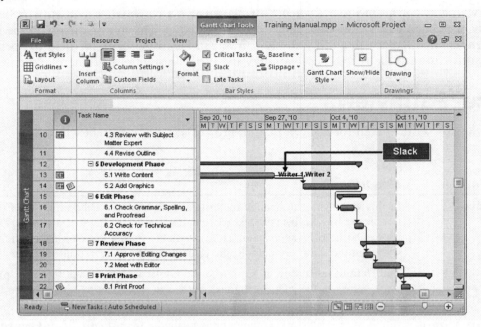

Figure 5-2: *A project with slack displayed.*

Project Optimization Methods

You can optimize your schedule in Microsoft Project by using a number of methods.

- Reduce the total slack in a project schedule by adjusting constraints or resources.
- Add resources to critical tasks in order to shorten the duration of the task.
- Replace resources of a critical task in order to move up the task start date.
- Divide critical tasks so that the work is split among resources and completed simultaneously.

How to Shorten a Project Using the Critical Path

Procedure Reference: View the Critical Path

To view the critical path:

1. View the project plan in the **Gantt Chart** or the **Detail Gantt** view.

 The **Gantt Chart Wizard** must be added to the Ribbon in Project 2010. Add the wizard by choosing **File→Options→Customize Ribbon.**

2. View the critical path for your plan.

   - On the Ribbon, on the **Format** tab, in the **Bar Styles** section, select **Critical Tasks.**
   - On the Ribbon, on the **View** tab, in the **Task Views** section, click **Network Diagram, Detail Gantt,** or **Gantt Chart.**
   - Use the **Gantt Chart Wizard.**

     a. Launch the **Gantt Chart Wizard** from the **Custom** tab you created when you added the **Gantt Chart Wizard** to the Ribbon.

     b. In the **Gantt Chart Wizard,** click **Next** to go to the next page.

     c. On the second page of the wizard, verify that the **Critical path** option is selected and click **Next** to specify that the critical tasks in the **Gantt Chart** should be highlighted and to move to the next page.

     d. On the third page of the wizard, verify that the **Resources and dates** option is selected and click **Next** to specify that the resources and the dates in the Gantt bars should be displayed and to move to the next page.

     e. On the fourth page of the wizard, verify that the **Yes** option is selected and click **Next** to specify that the link must be shown between dependent tasks and to move to the next page.

     f. Click **Format It** to apply the custom **Gantt Chart.**

     g. Click **Exit Wizard** to view the newly formatted **Gantt Chart.**

3. On the Ribbon, on the **View** tab, in the **Task Views** section, click **Network Diagram, Detail Gantt,** or **Gantt Chart** to review the critical path for the project and verify that the project will finish as scheduled.

Procedure Reference: Identify Slack in a Project Plan

To identify slack in a project plan:

1. Display the critical path in the **Gantt Chart** view or the **Detail Gantt** view.
2. On the Ribbon, on the **Format** tab, in the **Bar Styles** section, check the **Slack** check box.
3. In the **Gantt Chart,** identify the tasks that have slack displayed.
4. If necessary, on the **Task** tab, click the **Scroll to Task** button to view the Gantt bar for the task.

Procedure Reference: Display Total Slack in a Project Plan

To display the total slack for a project plan:

1. Display the **Gantt Chart** view.
2. In the entry table pane, from the **Add New Column** drop-down list, select **Total Slack.**

Procedure Reference: Divide Tasks

To divide tasks:

1. In the **Task Name** list, select a task to be divided into two tasks.
2. Select the text of the existing task, type the desired new task name, and press **Enter.**
3. In the **Duration** column, type the desired duration for the revised task and press **Enter.**
4. Insert a task row above the divided task to add another task.
5. Type the task name and duration for this newly created task.
6. If necessary, assign another resource to the divided task.
7. If necessary, adjust the task relationship between the divided tasks to **Start-to-Start** to shorten the project finish date.

Removing a Task

To remove a task from the project plan, select the row indicator for the task to be deleted and press **Delete.**

ACTIVITY 5-1
Optimizing the Schedule of a Project

Data Files:

C:\084602Data\Finalizing the Project\Training Manual.mpp

Scenario:

You have called for a status meeting with the Training Manual Project team because the project finish date must be adjusted. The senior management team would like the new Training Manual to be available to hand out to all employees at the next all employee meeting on Friday Oct, 1st. The first thing you need to do is to look at the critical path of your plan and to identify areas and tasks that can be adjusted to align with the new project finish date. Then, you need to make necessary adjustments to the project schedule to meet the updated project finish date.

---

1. Display the critical path in the **Gantt Chart.**

    a. Open the C:\084602Data\Finalizing the Project\Training Manual.mpp file.

    b. In the Training Manual.mpp file, on the Ribbon, on the **Format** tab, in the **Bar Styles** section, select **Critical Tasks.**

    c. Observe that the critical tasks are represented by red bars and noncritical tasks are represented by blue bars in the **Gantt Chart.**

    d. In the right pane, scroll to the right to view the entire critical path for the project.

    e. Verify that the current project finish date is 10/14.

---

2. Identify the slack time in the project.

    a. On the **Format** tab, select **Slack** to display the slack in the project.

    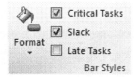

    b. Observe that the slack time is displayed in the **Gantt** view. Place the mouse pointer over the slack time for task 9.

    c. Notice the slack information displayed. The free slack time shows that there are 3 days of slack before the next linked task starts.

    d.   From the indicators column in the **Gantt Chart,** display the screentip for the constraint applied to task 10, **Review with Subject Matter Expert.**

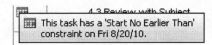

    e.   Because of the external Subject Matter Expert constraint applied to the linked task, you cannot adjust the slack time for task 9, **Present to Publisher.** Place the mouse pointer over the slack time for task 13, **Write Content.** There are 3 days of slack between the **Write Content** task and the **Add graphics** task that can be adjusted.

3.   Remove slack time from the schedule by adjusting the task 14 constraint.

    a.   In the **Task Entry** table, double-click task 14.

    b.   Click the **Advanced** tab, and from the **Constraint type** drop-down list, select **As Soon As Possible** to adjust the constraint on task 14.

    c.   Click **OK** to adjust the dates and remove the slack from the schedule.

4.   Divide task 13 into two separate tasks.

    a.   Select task 13.

    b.   Type *Write Lessons 1-5* and press **Enter.**

 The work breakdown numbers are automatically edited.

    c.   Verify that task 14 is selected and press **Insert** to insert a new task.

    d.   Type the task name as *Write Lessons 6-10* and press **Enter.**

    e.   In the **Duration** field for the new task, type *12.5* and press **Enter.**

5.   Remove the **Writer 2** resource from task 13 and assign it to task 14.

    a.   Select task 13.

    b.   Click and drag the divide bar to the right to view all the columns in the **Gantt Chart.**

    c.   On the Ribbon, click the **Resource** tab and then click **Assign Resources.**

    d.   In the **Resources from My Training Manual.mpp** section, select the **Writer 2** resource.

    e.   Click **Remove** to remove the second resource assigned to task **Write Lessons 1-5.**

    f.   In the **Assign Resources** dialog box, click **Close.**

    g.   Select the **Duration** column for task 13, type *12.5* and press **Enter.**

h.   Select task 14, **Write Lessons 6-10** and assign **Writer 2.**

| 5.1 Write Lessons 1-5 | 12.5 days | Wed 9/1/10 | Fri 9/17/10 | 11 | Writer 1 |
| 5.2 Write Lessons 1-6 | 12.5 days? | Mon 9/20/10 | Wed 10/6/10 | 13 | Writer 2 |

6.   Change the task relationship type so that both tasks occur simultaneously.

a.   Observe that the taskbars for both tasks are shown one after the other, indicating that the duration of the write content task has not been shortened.

b.   In the **Task Entry** table, select the **Predecessors** field for task 14, **Write Lessons 6–10.**

c.   In the **Predecessors** field for task 14, click after the number **13,** type *SS* and press **Enter.**

d.   Verify that the taskbars are shown as being completed simultaneously and that the finish date has moved up.

| 5.1 Write Lessons 1-5 | 12.5 days | Wed 9/1/10 | Fri 9/17/10 | 11 | Writer 1 |
| 5.2 Write Lessons 6-10 | 12.5 days | Wed 9/1/10 | Fri 9/17/10 | 13SS | |

e.   Save the file as *My Training Manual.mpp*

TOPIC B
Set a Baseline

In the previous topic, you made adjustments to the schedule based on a new project finish date. You can now consider your project plan to be finalized. However, before you begin tracking progress on the project, you will want to preserve your original project estimates so that you will have some data to compare the actual project results with. In this topic, you will set a project baseline.

Once your project begins, you will enter updated information into your plan as necessary that may not match the original plan information. As you make adjustments between the original plan and the actual project progress, such as task duration, start and finish dates, or costs, saving a project baseline becomes essential. Setting a baseline creates a benchmark for future reference, and can be referenced and tracked within the project file.

Baselines

Definition:

Baselines are original project plans used to monitor a project's progress. A baseline includes tasks, resources, assignments, and cost estimates. After you enter the complete project information in your project plan, you save a baseline plan, so that you can view the results in the task sheet view. The dates in the start and finish fields are copied to the baseline start and baseline finish fields, and so on for several fields. In effect, this saves a copy of the current date information for future reference.

Example:

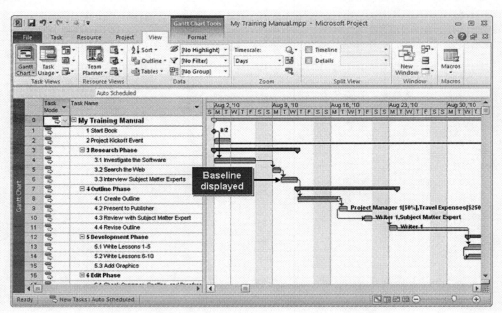

Figure 5-3: *A baseline displayed in Project.*

The Set Baseline Dialog Box

The **Set Baseline** dialog box is used to set a baseline plan or an interim plan for tasks, resources, and assignments, for the entire project, or selected tasks. You can set multiple baselines and have up to 11 different baselines for your project. You also have the option to update a baseline by rolling up subtasks into selected summary tasks or to all summary tasks within a project plan. The start and finish dates for tasks are updated as you adjust and track your project using baselines.

Figure 5-4: *Setting a baseline.*

Actual Progress

The *actual progress* of a task is the actual work completed for a specific task that gets updated by the project manager. This project information can be compared to a baseline in order to track overall project progress. The actual progress can be entered in the **Percent complete** text box in the **Task Information** dialog box or in the **Task Form.** In the **Gantt Chart,** the actual progress is represented by a thin black line on the Gantt bar.

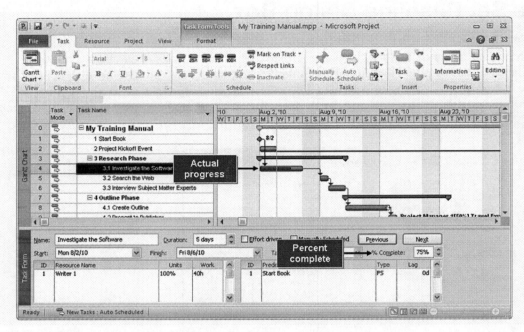

Figure 5-5: *Actual progress in the Gantt Chart.*

The Project Statistics Dialog Box

Once you set a baseline plan, the baseline statistics are displayed in the **Project Statistics** dialog box. The dialog box is used to review the scheduled timing and sequence of tasks within a project against the actual information that shows what has actually occurred. It shows the variance between the saved baseline plan and the current schedule of the start and finish dates, duration, work, and costs. It is accessed from the **Project Information** dialog box. The presence of baseline statistics generates variance statistics and displays them in the dialog box.

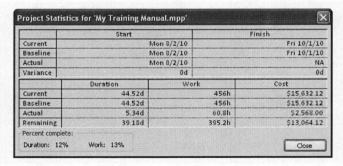

Figure 5-6: *Project statistics.*

How to Set a Baseline

Procedure Reference: Set a Baseline

To set a baseline:

1. On the **Project** tab, choose **Set Baseline→Set Baseline.**
2. In the **Set Baseline** dialog box, check **Set baseline** to set the baseline plan.
3. In the **For** section, select the baseline options.
   - Select **Entire project** to baseline the entire project or;
   - Select **Selected tasks** to baseline selected tasks in the plan and then select the desired **Roll up baselines** option.
     - Use **To all summary tasks** to baseline all summary tasks in the plan.
     - Use **From subtasks into selected summary task(s)** to baseline the subtasks in a summary task.
4. Click **OK** to set the baseline.
5. To view the baseline, on the **Format** tab, in the **Bar Styles** section, click **Baseline** and select the baseline to view from the list.

Procedure Reference: Clear a Baseline Plan

To clear a baseline plan:

1. On the **Project** tab, choose **Set Baseline→Clear Baseline.**
2. In the **Clear Baseline** dialog box, select the desired option to clear the baseline plan.
3. In the **For** section, select the desired option to clear the baseline plan as needed.
4. Click **OK** to clear the baseline.

Procedure Reference: Update Actual Progress

To update the actual progress of a plan:

1. View the project in one of the **Task Views.**
2. Update the percent complete.
   - Using the split view, select the task to edit in the **Task Entry** table, then in the **Task Form,** in the **% Complete** field, enter the percent.
   - In the **Task Entry** table, double-click the task to edit. On the **General** tab, in the **Percent complete** field, enter the percent.
3. View the actual progress in the desired view.

Procedure Reference: View Project Statistics

To view project statistics:

1. On the **Project** tab, click **Project information.**
2. In the **Project Information** dialog box, click **Statistics.**

ACTIVITY 5-2
Setting a Baseline Plan

Before You Begin:

The My Training Manual.mpp file is open.

Scenario:

With all the recent changes made to the Training Manual project, you would like to capture your project estimates so that you can later compare them with the actual project results. This will allow you to compare the actual project progress against the plan.

1. View the project statistics.

   a. On the Ribbon, click the **Project** tab and then click **Project Information.**

   b. In the **Project Information for 'My Training Manual.mpp'** dialog box, click **Statistics.**

   c. In the **Project Statistics for 'My Training Manual.mpp'** dialog box, observe that the **Baseline** and **Actual** rows in the **Start** and **Finish** columns read **NA,** indicating that a baseline has not yet been set and no progress has been entered.

	Start	Finish
Current	Mon 8/2/10	Thu 10/14/10
Baseline	NA	NA
Actual	NA	NA
Variance	0d	0d

	Duration	Work	Cost
Current	53.52d	656h	$20,132.12
Baseline	0d	0h	$0.00
Actual	0d	0h	$0.00
Remaining	53.52d	656h	$20,132.12

   d. Click **Close.**

2. Set a baseline plan.

   a. On the **Project** tab, choose **Set Baseline→Set Baseline.**

   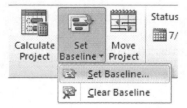

   b. In the **Set Baseline** dialog box, verify that the **Set baseline** option is selected and that in the **For** section, the **Entire project** option is selected.

    c.   Click **OK** to accept the defaults and set a baseline for the entire project.

3.   View the project baseline information in the **Gantt Chart.**

    a.   Click the **Format** tab.

    b.   In the **Bar Styles** section, click **Baseline** and select the most current baseline.

    c.   Notice the gray Gantt bars added to the **Gantt** view. You can compare the baseline against the current project.

4.   Enter the actual progress for the **Research Phase** of the project.

    a.   In the **Task Entry** table, select task 4, **Investigate the Software.**

    b.   Switch to the **Details** split view to display the **Task Form.**

    c.   On the **Task Form,** in the **% Complete** field, select the text and type *100%*

    d.   Click **OK** and then click **Next** to move to task 5, **Search the Web.**

    e.   In the **% Complete** field, select the text and type *75%*

    f.   Click **OK** and then click **Next** to move to task 6, **Interview Subject Matter Experts.**

    g.   In the **% Complete** field, select the text and type *10%* and then click **OK.**

    h.   On the **View** tab, in the **Split View** section, uncheck the **Details** check box.

5.   View the updated project information.

    a.   Display the **Project Statistics** dialog box.

    b.   Compare the **Baseline** information with the actual information entered.

    c.   Click **Close.**

    d.   Save the file.

TOPIC C
Print a Project Summary Report

In the previous topic, you finalized your project plan and saved a baseline plan for your project. With your project plan nearing completion, you may want to display, analyze, print, or distribute your project plan data to the necessary recipients. In this topic, you will print a project summary report.

Having your project plan on your computer's hard drive as a .mpp file will be extremely helpful to you. However, it is not a good format for presenting the project plan data to team members. It is more useful to print a view with a cost table applied, or generate a cost report to distribute to the group. Project offers a variety of built-in views and reports that can help you print and analyze project data.

Reports

Definition:

A *report* is a generated output from Project that is used to deliver specific project information. Basic reports are divided into six categories. You can change any of these reports to present the information that you want. If none of the default reports meet your information needs, you can use a template to create a custom basic report.

Example:

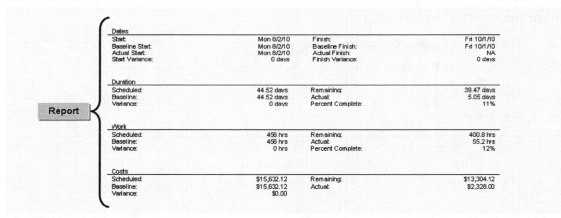

Figure 5-7: A sample report.

Report Types

The six different categories of reports in Project allow you to select the most appropriate format to display data.

Report Category	Description
Overview	 This category is used to select, edit, and generate a report to summarize the number of tasks, project costs, or to list the critical tasks or working times for each day. There are five standard report types in this category.
Current Activities	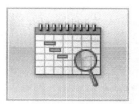 This category is intended for more frequent usage and geared toward audiences more directly involved with the tasks in the project. There are six standard reports in this category.
Costs	 This category is effective in tracking the budget cost of a project. There are five standard reports for reviewing your project's costs and budget.
Assignments	 This category is used to generate the to-do lists for resources and their assigned tasks, to follow up with resources and their current task progress, or to determine who has too many assignments in the available time. There are four standard reports in this category.

Report Category	Description
Workload	This category has excellent tracking tools for viewing the amount of work assigned to a task or per resource, on a weekly basis. There are two reports in this category.
Custom	This category is used to adapt an existing report, or create an entirely new report.

View Printing Options

Views are visual representations of the tasks or resources in a project that can be printed in various ways.

View	Allows You To
Timeline	Print the project's timeline view. You can add specific tasks to the timeline when needed or for a specific meeting or presentation. To print the timeline, it must be selected in the **Gantt Chart.**
Task Views	Print any of the project task views, such as **Gantt Chart, Task Usage, Network Diagram,** or **Calendar** by selecting the view and then choosing to print.
Resources Views	Print any of the resource views, such as **Team Planner, Resource Sheet,** or **Resource Usage** by selecting the view first and then choosing to print.

Print Settings

There are a number of print settings available on the **Print** page in the Backstage view. They include:

- Print Entire Project, which will print a project from start to finish.
- Print Specific Dates, which will print only the timescale between selected dates specified in the print settings.
- Print Specific Pages, which will print only the pages specified in the print settings.
- Print Custom Dates and Pages, which will print specific pages and timescale dates specified in the print settings.

Project File Format Options

There are a couple of file formats available to you to view Project information, including PDF and XPS files. To save project plan information as a PDF file, you use the **Save As** dialog box to generate the PDF in the desired location. To save as an XPS file, you use the **Print** page options available in the Backstage view to configure specific print settings and to select the Microsoft XPS Document Writer from the Printers list.

The XPS File Format

The XML Paper Specification (XPS) file format is similar to a Portable Document Format (PDF) file, in that it is a digital representation of the application-specific data. The XPS file keeps the source file's formatting and appearance. For more information on Microsoft's XPS document specification, visit **http://windows.microsoft.com/en-us/windows-vista/products/features/productivity**.

How to Print a Project Summary Report

Procedure Reference: Print a Project Summary Report

To print a project summary report:

1. On the **Project** tab, in the **Reports** section, click **Reports.**
2. In the **Reports** dialog box, click the icon of the report category you want to print.
3. Click **Select** to display the dialog box for the selected report category.
4. Click the icon of the report that you want to print.
5. Click **Select** to display the print preview of the report.
6. Click **Print** to print the report.
7. In the **Print** dialog box, click **OK** to print the report.

Procedure Reference: Print a View

To print a view:

1. In Project, select the view you want to print.
2. On the Ribbon, choose **File→Print.**
3. Configure the print settings needed and then click **Print.**

ACTIVITY 5-3
Printing a Project Summary Report

Before You Begin:
The My Training Manual.mpp file is open.

Scenario:
As the manager for the training manual project, you want to discuss the total cost of your project with your team. You also want to refer to the project summary information such as project start and finish dates, duration, work hours, and costs. You need to quickly refer to resource information, specifically who does what tasks when. To prepare for the meeting, you need to generate the correct report and set the printing options you need.

---

1. Display the **Gantt Chart** with the cost table applied.

    a. On the Ribbon, click the **View** tab.

    b. In the **Data** section, choose **Tables→Cost.**

    c. Widen columns in the **Gantt Chart** as necessary to view all the columns.

    d. Observe the total estimated current project cost.

---

2. Display the **Overview Reports.**

    a. On the Ribbon, click the **Project** tab.

    b. On the **Project** tab, click **Reports.**

    c. In the **Reports** dialog box, verify that **Overview** is selected.

    d. Click **Select** to display the **Overview Reports** dialog box, to view the various report types.

---

3. Preview the **Project Summary** report.

a.   In the **Overview Reports** dialog box, verify that **Project Summary** is selected.

b.   Click **Select** to display the print preview of the report to be printed.

c.   Click the report to zoom in and view its details.

d.   On the Ribbon, click the **File** tab to return to the project.

4.   Print the **Who Does What When** report for the last two weeks of the project to an XPS file.

a.   In the **Reports** dialog box, display the **Assignments** reports.

b.   Display the preview of the **Who Does What When** report.

c.   In the **Settings** list, select **Print Specific Dates.**

d.   In the **Dates** text box, select the current date and type *9/17/2010*

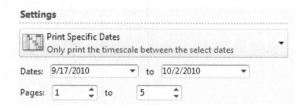

e.   Verify that the **Microsoft XPS Document Writer** option is selected and click **Print.**

f.   In the **Save the File As** dialog box, navigate to the C:\084602Data\Finalizing the Project folder and type *My Training Manual.xps* and then click **Save.**

g.   On the **File** tab, choose **Exit** to close the Project application.

Lesson 5 Follow-up

In this lesson, you finalized a project plan. The techniques presented in this lesson will help you avoid project delays, shorten your project duration, set a baseline for your project plan, and print and report your project data in the desired format. All these components ensure that your project finishes on time and that all reports are generated and delivered to the necessary recipients.

1. **What techniques might you use on the job to shorten a project's total duration?**

2. **In your experience, when will setting a baseline be helpful?**

Follow-up

In this course, you set up a functional project plan using Microsoft® Project 2010. By creating a project plan, organizing tasks within it, assigning resources, and finalizing the plan, you will be able to effectively manage project information, calculate and maintain a project schedule, track project costs, and analyze and communicate project data.

What's Next?

Microsoft® Project 2010: Level 2 is the next course in this series. In that course, you will build on the skills with creating project plans that you developed in this course by using those project plans to manage a project during project execution. In Level 2, you will update, monitor, modify, and customize your project plans in response to the changes and requirements of actual project work.

A | Additional Procedures to Create a Schedule in Microsoft Project 2010

Lesson Time: 15 minutes

Objectives:

In this lesson, you will identify additional methods to create a project schedule in Microsoft Project 2010.

You will:

● Identify how to create a project schedule from an existing project, an Excel workbook, and from a SharePoint task list.

TOPIC A

Additional Methods to Create a Project Schedule

How to Create a Project Schedule

Procedure Reference: Create a Project Schedule from an Existing Project

To create a new project schedule from an existing project:

1. Open Project 2010.
2. On the Ribbon, choose **File→New.**
3. In the **New from existing** section, click **New from existing project.**
4. Navigate to the location of the file you want to use to create a new project. Select the project file and click **Create New.**
5. On the Ribbon, choose **File→Save As.** Select the location for the new file and then specify a file name.
6. Edit the project information and specific dates for tasks as needed.

Procedure Reference: Create a New Project Schedule from an Excel Workbook

To create a new Project schedule from an Excel workbook:

1. Open Project 2010.
2. On the Ribbon, choose **File→New.**
3. In the **New from existing** section, double-click **New from Excel workbook.**
4. In the **Open** dialog box, navigate to the Excel workbook you want to use.

5. In the **Import Wizard,** on the **Welcome to the Project Import Wizard** page, click **Next.**

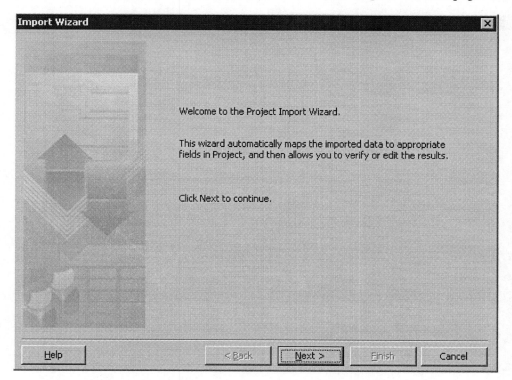

6. On the **Map** page, verify that **New map** is selected and click **Next.**

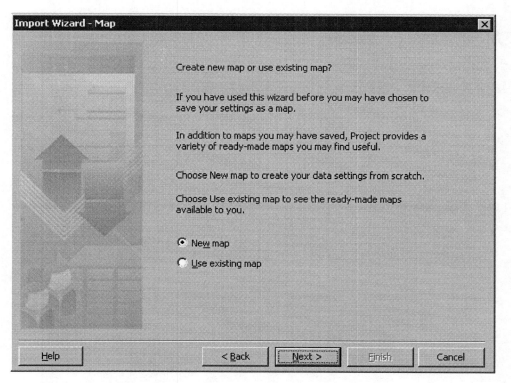

7. On the **Import Mode** page, verify that **As a new project** is selected and click **Next.**

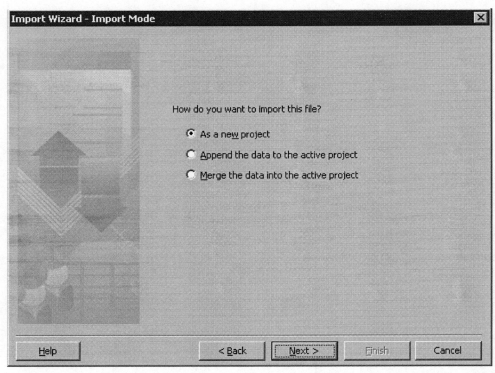

8. On the **Map Options** page, select the types of data and Excel options you prefer and then click **Next.**

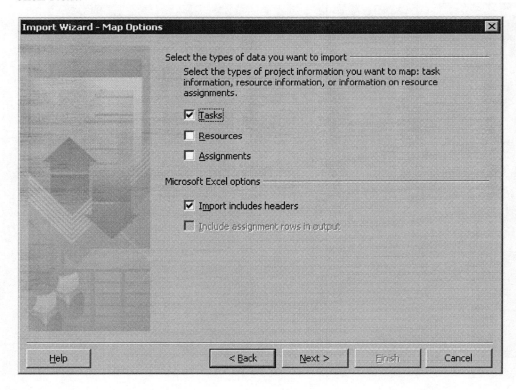

9. On the **Task Mapping** page, edit the fields as needed and click **Next,** then either save the map, or click **Finish.**

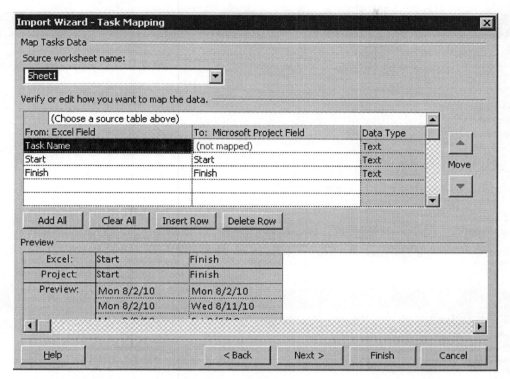

10. Review the project plan and save the file.

Procedure Reference: Create a Project Schedule from a SharePoint Task List

To create a new Project schedule from a SharePoint task list:

1. Launch the **SharePoint 2010** site.

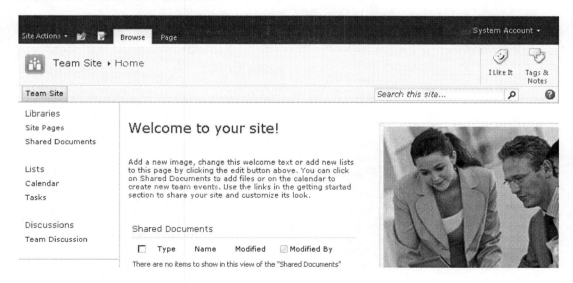

2. At the bottom of the sites' **Home** page, click the **All Site Content** link, navigate to **Create→List,** and click **Project Tasks.**

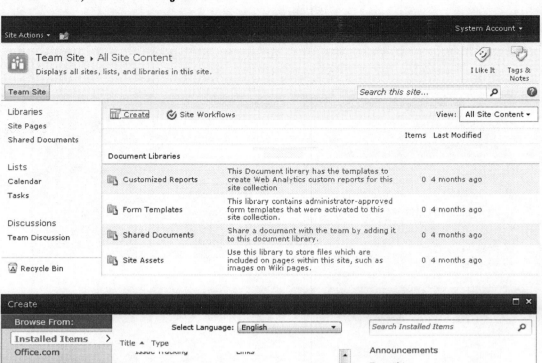

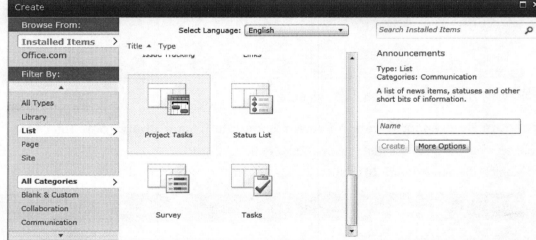

3. In the **Project Tasks** list, in the **Title** column, enter the Project tasks and then enter the start dates and the due dates for each task.

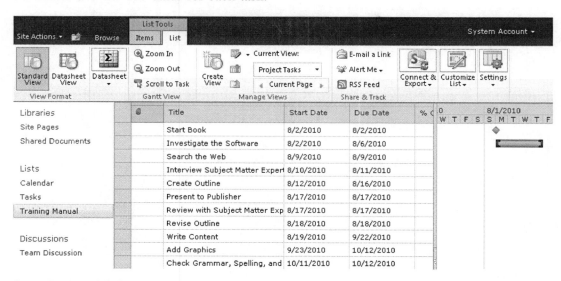

4. Open Project 2010.
5. On the Ribbon, choose **File→New.**
6. In the **New from existing** section, click **New from SharePoint task list.**
7. In the **Import SharePoint Tasks List** dialog box, enter the URL of the SharePoint site and select the project task list created and then click **OK.**

8. Review the project plan and save the file.

Lesson Labs

Lesson labs are provided as an additional learning resource for this course. The labs may or may not be performed as part of the classroom activities. Your instructor will consider setup issues, classroom timing issues, and instructional needs to determine which labs are appropriate for you to perform, and at what point during the class. If you do not perform the labs in class, your instructor can tell you if you can perform them independently as self-study, and if there are any special setup requirements.

Lesson 1 Lab 1

Displaying a Project in Various Views

Activity Time: 10 minutes

Data Files:

C:\084602Data\Getting Started\HTML Training Manual.mpp, C:\084602Data\Getting Started\ XML Training Manual.mpp

Scenario:

You have recently joined the project management team of an organization. In a week's time, you will be assigned your first project, and your supervisor has given you samples of various project plans from experienced project managers in your organization. As you are a novice to the Microsoft Project 2010 application, you decide to explore the software and get a feel for how the project tasks and resources are represented in the sample project plans. There are two samples provided to you—HTML Training Manual.mpp and XML Training Manual.mpp.

1. Launch the Microsoft Project 2010 application.

2. Open the HTML Training Manual.mpp file from the C:\084602Data\Getting Started folder in the default view.

3. Use screentips to identify any screen element that you are curious about.

4. Display the view where you will be able to review all the tasks and task dependencies in a tabular format.

5. Close the HTML Training Manual.mpp file.

6. Open the XML Training Manual.mpp file from the C:\084602Data\Getting Started folder in the default view.

7. On the **View** tab, use the **More Views** dialog box to display the **Resource Name Form** to view task entries, schedule, and work information about each resource.

8. Close the XML Training Manual.mpp file.

Lesson 2 Lab 1

Creating a New Workspace Project Plan

Activity Time: 20 minutes

Scenario:

As a project manager for Our Global Company, you are assigned to oversee an initiative the company is undertaking to renovate office space in the company's headquarters. You will need to create a project plan for the new workspace project. Microsoft Project is Our Global Company's standard project-management tool. You have the following general information about your project:

- Subject: Refurbish New Offices
- Manager: *Your Name*
- Company: Our Global Company
- Project start date: September 1, 2010

Also, you would like to summarize your project, and you have identified the various tasks with their duration and the resources involved in the project. The details are listed below.

- Initial Milestone: Project Start
- Paint the Walls: 2 days
- Install Partitions: 1 day
- Install Network Cables: 3 days
- Lay Carpet: 2 days
- Prepare Offices: 5 days
- Assemble Furniture: 2 days
- Hook up Computers: 1 day
- Move in Belongings: 2 days
- Project End: 0 day
- Resources: Laborer, Painters 1 and 2, and Technician

1. Generate a new project plan.

2. Use the **Project Information** dialog box to enter the project start date as *9/1/2010.*

3. Save the new project file as *My New Workspace.mpp.*

4. Enter the project information on the **Summary** tab of the project properties dialog box.

5. Enter the project tasks, milestones, and duration.

6. Display the initial project summary task.

7. If necessary, expand the columns of the view to display the column data.

8. Enter the resource information.

9. Save and close the file.

Lesson 3 Lab 1

Organizing Tasks in a Project Plan

Activity Time: 20 minutes

Data Files:

C:\084602Data\Managing Tasks\New Workspace.mpp

Scenario:

You have a project plan, New Workspace.mpp, which includes tasks and duration. Now, you are ready to make some organizational adjustments to these tasks to improve the clarity, usability, and overall effectiveness of the plan. You realize that certain tasks can be converted to subtasks to enable viewing the hierarchy of the various tasks. You plan to have a staff meeting for 1 hour every week on Mondays from September 1, 2010 to November 1, 2010. To determine the project timeline, you decide to link all milestones and subtasks using the default relationship. You then need to modify the relationship between similar tasks so that they can start at the same time. You want to park a reminder to check cable wires for the task **Install Network Cables.** You also realize that the painters are only available on October 7th and 8th. As a project manager, you have to ensure that the project finishes as scheduled; so you set a target date for the completion of the task **Move in Belongings** as October 24, 2010.

1. Open the New Workspace.mpp file and indent the tasks **Assemble Furniture, Hook up Computers,** and **Move in Belongings** as subtasks of the task **Prepare Offices.**

2. Display the outline numbers for the newly indented tasks.

3. Link all milestones and subtasks in a finish-to-start relationship.

4. Change the task relationship between the tasks **Install Partitions** and **Install Network Cables** to a start-to-start relationship.

5. Add the weekly recurring task, **Staff Meeting.**

6. Set a constraint for the task, **Paint the Walls.**

7. Set a deadline for the task, **Move in Belongings.**

8. Add task notes for the task, **Install Network Cables.**

9. Save the file as *My New Workspace.mpp* and close the plan.

Lesson 4 Lab 1

Managing Resources in the New Workspace Project Plan

Activity Time: 15 minutes

Data Files:

C:\084602Data\Managing Resources\New Workspace.mpp

Scenario:

As the project manager for the new workspace project, you have spent most of the month of September in purchasing materials, lining up contractors and various labor resources, and confirming the delivery dates. Due to some unavoidable reasons, the laborer can work only in the afternoons (1:00 to 5:00). You received the cost information for the resources and the tasks these resources would perform. You need to enter this information in your project plan. Also, you want to ensure that none of the resources in the plan are overallocated. The following list provides the details about the tasks performed by the resources and their cost information.

- Paint the Walls: Painter 1
- Install Partitions: Laborer
- Install Network Cables: Technician
- Lay Carpet: Laborer
- Assemble Furniture: Laborer
- Hook up Computers: Technician
- Move in Belongings: Laborer
- Laborers' charge: $50 per hour
- Technicians' charge: $100 per hour
- Painters' charge: $65 per hour

1. Open the New Workspace.mpp file and create a resource calendar for the laborer resource.

2. Assign the resources to their tasks.

3. Assign the laborer as a second resource to the **Install Network Cables** task because the technician needs some unskilled assistance for fixing the network cables.

4. Assign Painter 2 to the **Paint the Walls** task because the Painter 1 resource needs skilled assistance for painting the walls.

5. Enter the cost information for the resources.

6. Use a view of your choice to check all resources to determine if any are overallocated.

7. Save the file as *My New Workspace.mpp.*

8. Level the entire resource pool.

9. Save and close the file.

Lesson 5 Lab 1
Finalizing a Project

Activity Time: 15 minutes

Data Files:

C:\084602Data\Finalizing the Project\New Workspace.mpp

Scenario:

You finished the planning phase of your project plan, New Workspace.mpp. You notice that the current end date is unacceptable because a notice sent out to employees stated an earlier move in date of October 22nd. The management team has provided you with an additional Laborer resource that is available to work full time. You are also notified by the painting company that the painters will be finishing on October 7th, instead of October 8th. With these updates, you need to make the necessary changes to the project schedule to pull in the project finish date. Once you have updated the project plan, you need to save the original plan and the preview the **Project Summary** report.

1. Open the New Workspace.mpp plan and view the critical path and the project finish date.

2. Add Laborer 2 to the **Resource Sheet** and update the resource cost information.

3. Assign Laborer 2 to the **Assemble Furniture, Move in Belongings, Install Network Cables,** and **Lay the Carpet** tasks.

4. Update the **Paint the Walls** task with the new finish date.

5. Verify that the end date has changed.

6. Save and view the baseline for the entire project.

7. Preview the **Project Summary** report.

8. Save the file as *My New Workspace.mpp* and close the file.

Solutions

Lesson 2

Activity 2-4

2.   **What screen changes occurred as a result of entering the task duration?**

   ✓ a) The summary task start and finish dates reflect the task duration.

   ✓ b) The active cell is automatically shifted to the next row.

   ✓ c) The length of the taskbar in the Gantt Chart increases to represent the duration.

     d) A Calendar icon is displayed in the indicators column of the selected task.

Glossary

actual progress
The actual work completed for a specific task that is updated by a project manager.

base calendars
A template that is used to schedule the standard working and nonworking time for a set of resources.

baselines
The original project plans used to monitor a project's progress.

budget resource
The project-level work, material, and cost resources that track the maximum capacity for a project to consume money, work, or material units.

cell
The intersection of a table row and column, where data is stored.

constraints
The conditions or limitations placed on the start or finish date of a task in a project plan.

cost resources
The miscellaneous expenses that vary from task to task and that are independent of the amount of work performed on the task.

critical path
The series of tasks that determine the calculated start date or finish date of a project.

critical tasks
The tasks on a critical path.

deadline
A target date indicating when you want a task to be completed.

duration
The time interval between the start and end time of a task.

effort-driven scheduling
A method used to determine the duration of a task based on the amount of effort available and applied to that task.

field
A location in a sheet, form, or chart that contains a specific kind of information about a task, a resource, or an assignment.

free slack
The amount of time a task can slip before it delays another task.

lag time
A delay between two dependent tasks.

lead time
The overlap between two tasks that are linked by a dependency.

leveling
The process of delaying or splitting tasks to resolve conflicts.

material resource
The supplies or other consumable items used to complete tasks in a project.

Microsoft SharePoint
A server-based collaboration software program from Microsoft.

milestone
A task with a zero duration that acts as a reference point marking a major project event.

outlining
The process of creating a hierarchical structure in a project that shows how tasks can be delegated to various levels.

overallocated resource
A resource that is scheduled to work beyond its capacity.

part-time resource
A resource scheduled to work less than 40 hours in a work week.

predecessor
A task that determines the start time of dependent tasks.

project calendar
The base calendar that specifies the default working and nonworking times for a project.

project management
The application of knowledge, skills, tools, and techniques to project activities to meet the requirements of a project.

project manager
The individual who is responsible for accomplishing the goals in a project by ensuring that work activities are completed as required on time, with quality and within budget.

project summary task
The highest level of work in a project that represents the project goal or project objective.

recurring task
A task that occurs repeatedly at regular intervals during the course of a project.

report
A format for generating project information that is appropriate for distribution.

resource allocation
The amount of time a resource is allocated to tasks and projects.

resource calendar
A calendar created to specify the working and nonworking times for an individual resource when exceptions from the base calendar exist.

resources
The people, equipment, material, and other miscellaneous items used to complete the tasks.

Ribbon
A panel at the top portion of the interface that contains a selection of commands to work on a Project file.

ScreenTip
A description of the task performed by a tool that appears when the mouse pointer is placed over the tool.

slack
The amount of time a task can slip before it affects another task's dates or the project finish date.

split view
A view that displays two views, with the view either in the bottom pane showing detailed information about the data selected, or in the top pane showing the project's timeline.

subtask
A task that contains the detailed steps necessary to complete summary tasks. Subtasks are represented in the Gantt Chart by blue bars.

successor
A task that is dependent on a predecessor task.

summary task
A task that contains the broad concepts of projects. Summary tasks are represented in the Gantt Chart by black bars with black triangular terminators.

table

A format that displays different fields of data for tasks and resources within a sheet view.

task calendar

A calendar applied to an individual task created to control the scheduling of a task when exceptions from the base calendar exist.

Task Inspector

A pane that provides information on factors affecting a specific task and can be used to track schedule changes.

task notes

The additional or supporting information that is added to a task.

task

An individual work item that defines to complete a project.

timescale

The range of time within which work has elapsed.

total slack

The amount of time a task can slip before it delays the project finish date.

unit

The representation of the percentage of a resource's time assigned to a task.

work breakdown structure

A hierarchy of tasks in a project represented by alphanumeric codes that identify each task's unique place in the structure.

work resource

The people or equipment used to complete tasks in a project.

work

The total amount of person-hours required to complete the resource's assignment.

Index

project optimization methods, 120

R

report types, 133
reports, 132
resource allocation, 107
resources, 50
  assigning, 97
  budget, 51
  cost, 51
  entering, 52
  entering a budget resource, 53
  entering costs, 103
  entering values for budget resources, 104
  material, 51
  resolving conflicts, 110
  sorting, 53
  work, 50
Ribbon, 6
Ribbon tabs, 7

S

ScreenTips, 6
slack, 108
  free, 119
  identifying, 121
  total, 119
split view, 96
  assigning resources, 98
subtasks, 38
successors, 65

T

tables, 24
Task Inspector, 74
task notes, 80
task variables, 95
tasks, 37
  adding a recurring task, 84
  adding notes, 81
  adding tasks to a project plan, 39
  critical, 118
  dividing, 122
  linking dependent tasks, 68
  modifying task relationship types, 68
  outlining tasks, 62
  project summary, 38
  recurring, 83
  summary, 38
times
  adding lag or lead time, 68
  lag, 66
  lead, 66
timescales, 12
  changing, 26

U

units, 45

W

work, 46
work breakdown structures, 60